HOLY ROVER

HOLY ROVER

JOURNEYS IN SEARCH OF MYSTERY, MIRACLES, AND

GOD

LORI ERICKSON

261
ERICKSON

HOLY ROVER
Journeys in Search of Mystery, Miracles, and God

Cover images: Image of Bear Butte in South Dakota by Chad Coppess/SD Tourism. Middle photo by joyt/Adobe Stock. Image of Machu Picchu in Peru by Eric Lindberg.

Cover design: Brad Norr

ISBN: 978-1-5064-2071-4
eBook ISBN: 978-1-5064-2072-1

For Jackie,
for Rich,
and most of all for Bob

THE WAY IT IS

There's a thread you follow. It goes among
things that change. But it doesn't change.
People wonder about what you are pursuing.
You have to explain about the thread.
But it is hard for others to see.
While you hold it you can't get lost.
Tragedies happen; people get hurt
or die; and you suffer and get old.
Nothing you do can stop time's unfolding.
You don't ever let go of the thread.

William Stafford

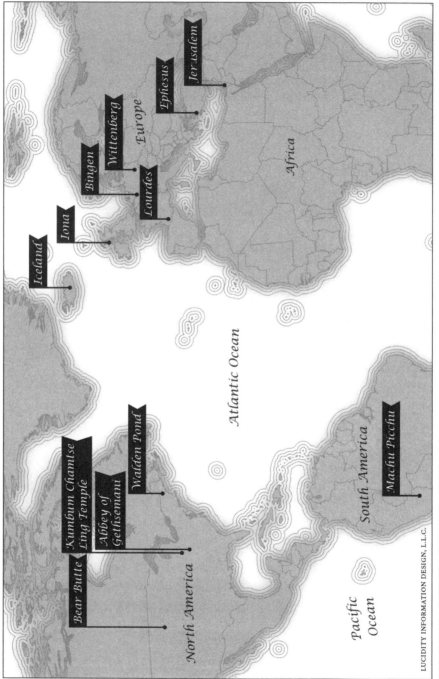

BOB CRONAN, LUCIDITY INFORMATION DESIGN, LLC

TABLE OF CONTENTS

TABLE OF CONTENTS

PROLOGUE

A FARMER'S DAUGHTER
ON THE BANK OF THE NILE

I'm sitting on the top deck of a boat docked on the bank of the Nile. Earlier in the day I'd toured its ancient temples in brilliant sun and fierce heat, but the evening brought air that was blessedly cooler, as soft as a pashmina shawl against my skin. A full moon hangs above the city, illuminating the outlines of dust-colored buildings. As stars multiply in the velvet sky above, I savor the scene below me, one that has changed little in thousands of years.

And I find myself wondering: how did an Iowa farmer's daughter get here?

The short answer is that I fell in love with pilgrimages, the sacred journeys that can begin in any corner of the world and eventually lead to Jerusalem, or Lourdes, or Machu Picchu, or to a boat docked on the bank of the Nile.

The long answer is this book.

My passion for pilgrimage springs from a fascination with religion in all its many weird and wonderful permutations. What makes some people handle snakes and others fast for Lent? How do Mormons get young people to devote two years of their lives to knocking on the doors of strangers? What's it like to go to Mecca? Why do Orthodox churches have those slightly scary looking icons? Do Trappist monks ever burst out laughing in the middle of the Great Silence? Do many people really believe that pieces of the True Cross exist? Why do people crawl on their knees to the Shrine of Our Lady of Guadalupe in Mexico City? What do nuns wear under their habits and Buddhist monks under their robes? All of it, the big and little questions, intrigue me.

In my search for the holy, I've wandered down many paths. I've been a Lutheran, a Wiccan, a Unitarian Universalist, a Buddhist, an Episcopalian, and an admirer of Native American traditions. I've been spiritual-but-not-religious and religious-but-not-spiritual. I can read tarot cards and balance chakras. My spirit animal is a bear, which is a great relief because for years I thought it was a raccoon, an animal that while perfectly fine lacks a certain gravitas.

After many years of spiritual wandering, I'm now a committed Christian, but one who frequently flirts with other religious traditions. I like to think I'm in an open marriage with Jesus—we're both free to spend time with other faiths, but at the end of the day we always come home to each other.

Through it all, the spiritual practice that's most shaped me is pilgrimage. My journeys have given me essential keys to understanding what was happening in my inner life. They've challenged my assumptions, forced me to confront my fears and prejudices, and deepened my faith. Among other changes, they eventually led me to become a writer specializing in spiritual travels and to ordination as a deacon in the Episcopal Church.

This book describes not a single pilgrimage, such as a six-month trip along the Pacific Crest Trail or the Camino de Santiago, but instead a dozen shorter ones. I think my experiences mirror those of many travelers today, people who don't have time for an extended retreat or journey, but who still feel a yearning for something more than the ordinary routines of work and family and the pleasures of a week at Disneyland.

I hope in reading about my pilgrimages, you'll be inspired to make your own, whether you're Christian, Jewish, Muslim, Buddhist, Hindu, or someone who kinda-sorta thinks there might be something more to ordinary reality than is immediately obvious.

A warning: once you set out on trips to holy places, if you're paying attention at all, your life will change.

❧

This may appear to be a trivial detail, but it's actually a key part of my story: I grew up on a dairy farm. This meant that we never traveled, because cows need to be milked twice a day.

My family never went anywhere for other reasons as well, including the fact that my parents didn't have much money, and they weren't the sort of people who'd have traveled even if they did have it. To them it was mystifying that anyone would want to leave home for pleasure. Think of the multiple ways things could go wrong, including restaurants where we didn't know what to order and food that could upset our stomachs. More serious dangers lurked, too. Early in their marriage my parents took a trip to the Wisconsin Dells, where my dad was stung by a bee on his face. That's just the sort of thing that could happen again if we ventured very far afield.

And the roads! My hometown of Decorah (population 8,000) was busy enough, but traveling involved driving on highways with more than two lanes. I remember how scared I was riding in the back seat of our car on my first trip to Minneapolis, where my sister had recently moved. My mother drove down an entry ramp onto the interstate and then stopped, waiting until all three lanes were completely clear before venturing out. I was startled to see people cursing at our car, because I'd never witnessed such rudeness in my quiet, well-mannered town.

My childhood was, in its own way, almost nineteenth-century. In the early years of my parents' marriage, my father farmed with horses.

I grew up without indoor plumbing and can vividly recall the thrill at the age of 11 of taking a shower *inside* the house. I was 16 before I stayed in a hotel, courtesy of a high school field trip. My family occasionally had dinner at Decorah's A&W Root Beer stand, but otherwise we didn't eat out. I recall long summers when the only excitement was a once-a-week trip to town, where I visited the public library and stocked up on books.

This may sound like a woe-is-me litany, but it isn't, because I had a happy childhood. I never doubted for a minute that I was loved by my parents and older sister and brother. I lived in an idyllic part of the world, a place with ample beauty and strong bonds of community.

I was also, to use the current jargon, free-range. I knew every square foot of our farm and spent endless hours exploring our woods and making up imaginary games in a playhouse I built under a stand of boxelder trees. The barn had a never-ending supply of kittens to play with before they got sick, lost, or run-over. Inside the house, I had my long-suffering cat Butterball, whom I dressed up in doll clothes for more years than was probably healthy for either her or me.

Every adventure I've had as an adult—the trips to holy sites near and far—I experience through the lens of this childhood. It was an ideal preparation for a life of wandering and wondering.

∽✢∾

Growing up, my most influential friend had been dead for 40 years by the time I met him.

We got together on Sundays at my grandparents' house. As the adults visited, I disappeared into a set of books kept on a shelf in a corner of the living room. The faux red-leather volumes of the *John L. Stoddard Lectures* were written by a Victorian adventurer who traveled the world from Boston to Bombay. He delivered reports of his travels to packed lecture houses throughout America and then turned his presentations into books. I read each of these volumes over and over again, their musty, moldy smell floating up to my nose each time I turned a page.

Thanks to Stoddard, I learned that traveling to Spain was so dangerous that people should prepare by visiting a priest for absolution, a doctor for medicine, and a lawyer to make a will. In Jerusalem, I joined him in shuddering at the sight of lepers begging in the streets. In Kyoto, we marveled together at dancing geishas, their dark, elaborately coiffed hair shining like a raven's wing.

Stoddard had a boundless enthusiasm for whatever he saw, and it thrilled me even from the distance of a century. In describing an Austrian cathedral, for example, he wrote:

> Today, perhaps, the mournful grandeur of the requiem yields to the joyous splendor of the nuptial mass—where bright eyes and resplendent gems relieve the somber shadows of the church with the warm glow of youth and radiance of love; and these again tomorrow may give place to some display of gorgeous vestments, flashing in the light of countless tapers, when a distinguished prelate shall be consecrated, or one of Austria's sovereigns be crowned.

I wasn't sure exactly what that meant, but I knew it must be splendid. Even more than the breathless prose, I loved the photographs and engravings. The sepia-toned illustrations showed worlds removed from me by time as well as distance. I knew that these places had changed since Stoddard had traveled there, but in some mysterious way I felt that they were still intact and that if I stared at the images long enough, I could stand on the Palace Quay in St. Petersburg or climb aboard an elephant in India.

Looking back, it was John L. Stoddard who turned me into a travel writer, though it would be years before I'd get the chance to follow in his footsteps. In my own writing I try to avoid his insensitivities (for example, unlike him, I've never used the phrase "idol-worshipping, ignorant natives"). But what he did then is what I do now: experience faraway places and then tell other people about them.

There's another curious thing about Stoddard, something that makes me wonder if there's not some karmic connection between the two of us. Raised as a Protestant and at one point a seminarian, he was an agnostic for 30 years before becoming a Roman Catholic. He wrote a book about his conversion called *Rebuilding a Lost Faith*, a work of apologetics that was popular for many years.

I suspect something happened to Stoddard that also happened to me: when you travel, your heart and soul open. And that's when the real journey starts.

❧

Several years ago, I got an email from my friend Marian. "Come with me to Istanbul," she wrote. "You can't call yourself a spiritual travel writer without visiting there."

"Actually, I've already been there with my friend John Stoddard," I wrote back. "But I'd love to go again."

I felt his presence most strongly on a cruise we took on the Bosphorus. Bundled against the cold, I watched as the major landmarks of the city passed by, recalling how Stoddard had been enchanted by them. I could see the outlines of Hagia Sophia and the Blue Mosque and the opulent palaces where sultans once dined overlooking the water.

And after we docked, as we exited the boat into the bustling commerce of the centuries-old Spice Bazaar, for a moment I swear I saw a tweed-clad Victorian gentleman ahead of me, walking with a gold-tipped cane. He looked back at me with a half-smile on his face, clearly glad to see me again, and then he disappeared into the crowd.

Martin Luther statue in Eisleben, Germany

CHAPTER 1

AMONG THE LUTHERANS

If you want to change the world, pick up your pen and write.

Martin Luther

~ PILGRIMAGE ~
Martin Luther Sites in Germany

Once when I was visiting my parents, I mentioned an article I'd read about the rarity of blue eyes. "Less than one percent of all the people who've ever lived have had them," I said.

My mother made the snorting noise that is her most potent form of disapproval. "That's not right," she said. "It's at least half."

And in her world, she was right. Decorah, a small town in northeast Iowa, was settled by Norwegian immigrants in the 1850s. It's clung proudly to that identity ever since. The entire town is marinated in Norse-ness, from the gnome-like *nisse* peeking out the windows of many homes to Nordic Fest, the annual celebration of Norwegian culture and traditions.

In the Decorah of my youth, status depended upon how closely you adhered to the platonic ideal of Norwegianhood. A local pastor's family, for example, had a singing group, like the Von Trapps only they dressed up in Norwegian folk costumes instead of German ones. They were all impossibly talented and photogenic (rumor had it that they had given up two of their children for adoption because they weren't sufficiently blonde). It also helped if you were part of the founding families of Luther College, the town's liberal arts bastion affiliated with the Lutheran Church. Even if your blood wasn't pure, you could still fake it by dressing up in colorful ethnic outfits for Nordic Fest, held on one of the hottest weekends of the year despite that being the type of weather least like that in Norway.

Thankfully, my own bloodline was untainted, as all of my great-grandparents came from Norway. The cultural traditions remained so strong that both of my parents grew up in homes where Norwegian was nearly as common as English. Naturally, we were Lutheran, as was virtually everyone I knew as a child.

Along with other blue-eyed Lutherans, we attended a church near our farm about ten miles from town. Constructed from limestone that its members quarried themselves, it had a tall steeple that could be seen for miles across the surrounding fields of corn and soybeans. It must have cost the frugal farmers in the parish a considerable amount of money to build it in the 1870s, which is an indication of the importance of people's religious faith to their lives.

During my childhood, the parish was filled with the descendants of those farmers, hard-working men of few words, my father among them. (Here's my favorite joke about these farmers, told in its entirety: "Did you hear the one about the husband who loved his wife so much he almost told her?") They showed up in church nearly every Sunday when they weren't planting or harvesting, but their religious enthusiasm was kept well under wraps. On Sunday mornings I was fascinated by one of our neighbors in particular, a farmer who nodded off as soon as the pastor started his sermon. His wife would dig her elbow into his ribs periodically, but he never stayed awake for long, dozing peacefully until the final hymn, at which time he would rise refreshed, having fulfilled his duty to God and his wife for another week.

In attending Sunday School as a young girl at this church, I learned three important things. One was that Jesus loved children, which I knew from the many pictures of him in a white robe, smiling as little boys and girls in 1950s clothes gathered around him. The second was that I should never marry a Catholic because if I was giving birth and it came to a choice between letting the baby die or letting the mother die, Catholics always wanted to save the baby. And third, I needed to memorize a lot of Bible verses so that if I was ever in a situation without any books—say if I was being held by the North Vietnamese—I would be so grateful to have lots of the Bible memorized to give me comfort and help me in my time of need.

As I grew older, my understanding of the Lutheran faith matured, though there were still some rough spots. For example, I was surprised to learn that Martin Luther, the founder of our church, was German. *How could this be?* I wondered. The only Lutherans I knew were Norwegian. It would have been acceptable, though not ideal, if he'd been Swedish or Danish—people who were a little foreign but still Scandinavian. But German? His nationality was an embarrassment, a stain on an otherwise unblemished biography. It wasn't dwelled upon in Sunday School classes, thankfully, as the primary focus was Luther's triumph over Catholic corruption, his emphasis on faith over works, his love of music, and his fondness for memorization.

In this Lutheran world, confirmation was nearly as important as marriage, a solemn rite for which we prepared by attending classes with the pastor on Wednesday evenings. He was approaching retirement by the time I started these classes, and parents took turns sitting in the back to make sure he was teaching us properly, listening and watching intently like judges during the Olympics. My parents didn't do that, of course, as they'd never have dreamed they knew better than a pastor. But obviously other parents were worried—exactly about what, I wasn't sure, but it had something to do with the fact that religion was very important and very serious.

After two years of classes, I was confirmed at age 13, which meant I could finally partake of communion: a thin wafer that tasted nothing like bread and wine served in little cups on a silver tray. That first Sunday I was nervous, as I'd been told the wafer was hard to swallow unless you'd prepared yourself by having a lot of saliva in your mouth (I didn't think that was very reverent, even though the pastor had recommended it). Goodness knows that if I started to cough, that little cup of liquid wouldn't help much. But I took my first communion without a hitch, and afterwards there was a party at our house, at which people gave me cards filled with money that I was to use for something worthwhile (and not buy a pet monkey, like my cousin had done with her confirmation money).

The first ripple of diversity in my religious life came when a cousin of mine married a Catholic, much to the disapproval of the relatives. "The problem with Catholics," my mom said darkly, "is they think they can go to confession and be forgiven for *anything*." Which led me to wonder, what were those Catholics doing? I knew they drank more than we did—Lutherans could drink privately, but I'd heard that Catholics drank at parties, right in front of everyone. I guessed a lot of confessions involved alcohol.

This prohibition against Catholicism was so engrained that I felt a delicious frisson of naughtiness the first time I went to mass with a Catholic friend. I was fascinated by how different it was. Instead of happy Jesus, surrounded by children, he was on a crucifix, looking sad. The church seemed huge and dark and mysterious, and it had a side altar dedicated to the Virgin Mary, even though as a Lutheran I knew the only time we were supposed to pay attention to her was during Advent and Christmas. The stained glass windows depicted saints with names I didn't know, and the entire church had an unfamiliar scent that I now recognize as incense, instead of the slightly antiseptic smell of Lutheran churches.

Given the Lutheran attitude towards Catholicism, it came as a terrible shock one Sunday in our country church when the word "catholic" suddenly appeared in the Apostle's Creed:

I believe in the Holy Spirit,
the holy catholic church, [instead of *Christian* church, as we had
   always said before]
the communion of saints,
the forgiveness of sins,
the resurrection of the body,
and the life everlasting. Amen.

Even though my parents weren't sensitive to theological nuances, they shared in the general dismay at this change. Oh, the pastor tried to explain it by saying there was a big difference between a small "c" (meaning universal) and a big "C" (meaning Roman Catholic), and the change in wording had nothing to do with expressing allegiance to the pope and we weren't going to be kneeling or praying to the Virgin Mary now or in the future, but there was nevertheless something deeply disturbing about this alteration in what we'd been saying since time immemorial, or at least since the church's services started being conducted in English instead of Norwegian.

It wasn't too long after this that yet another innovation was instituted: the passing of the peace, during which people were expected to greet those sitting next to them. This directive wasn't received very enthusiastically either, though at least it didn't imply outright heresy, as the change in the creed did. When that time in the service came, people stuck out their hands to their neighbors in the pew with eyes lowered, pulling them back quickly for fear of initiating a conversation:

"Peace be with you."

"Ja, you too."

The Lutheran church of my childhood had definite ways-of-doing-things that didn't have to be articulated, because everyone knew what they were. Church suppers had to include white buns with a slice of ham and American cheese, plus an array of "salads," as they were loosely termed, of various brilliant shades of Jell-O. After school was out for the summer, we attended Vacation Bible School, which turbocharged our memorizing (I got extra praise for being able to recite all the books of the Bible, reeling them off so fast that no individual names could be distinguished). And after we graduated from high school, many of us went to Lutheran colleges, where we could find another Lutheran to marry, thus escaping the dreaded possibility of ending up in a hospital one day trying to decide whether to kill ourselves or the baby.

In this world, being well-behaved was of paramount importance. I was, excessively so, earning good grades throughout my growing up years and pleasing my teachers so much that when I graduated from high school I was named Girl Citizen, an honor voted upon by the faculty and given to one girl from each graduating class. There was a Boy Citizen, too, making us a matched set. I wasn't entirely sure why

I received the honor, but I knew it had a lot to do with being nice to everyone, all the time. I'd achieved the equivalent of Eagle Scout rank in being a Good Girl.

As night follows day and summer spring, I, along with a good share of my graduating class, enrolled in Luther College. By then my mother was working in the college's cafeteria, and one of the perks of the job was free tuition. I received an excellent education there, one that taught me how to read critically, write well, and learn for myself. Because it's a Lutheran school, we had chapel several days a week, and during those services and in my classes I was introduced to a more mature form of the faith of my childhood.

But looking back, I can see how Lutheranism never truly took root in me. Because it was in the very air I breathed from the time I was born, it never had any mystery for me—and a search for mystery is what would soon start me on a lifetime of spiritual journeying. Like a character in a fairy tale, I've had to journey far to discover the treasures hidden close to home.

My college years were also circumscribed by the fact I never fit in socially. I wish I'd known about the universality of this feeling much earlier in my life, as it certainly would have saved some anxiety through the years. But when I was in college, everyone else appeared to be more sophisticated and worldly than me, especially the legions of tanned and athletic girls from the Twin Cities suburbs. They'd traveled widely and been cheerleaders and tennis players in their high schools. They knew how to wear make-up. And they weren't at Luther because their mothers worked in food service.

My college years passed, and despite walking by Martin Luther's statue every day on my way across campus, the faith of my childhood gradually slipped away.

My Lutheran Gordian Knot

Instead of writing about my childhood, I probably should just tell you to listen to reruns of Garrison Keillor's "News from Lake Wobegon." In describing small town Lutheranism in the upper Midwest, he's cornered the market on stories about hot dish suppers in church basements and taciturn Norwegian bachelor farmers (a redundancy, I realize). These are my people, God love 'em. I'm glad someone has chronicled their culture for posterity.

But in the midst of all the folksy nostalgia I admit to a certain ambivalence about my hometown. Whenever people hear I'm from Decorah, I've grown accustomed to their response: "Oh, what a nice town!" For years I agreed aloud and dissented privately, because stating that you aren't enthusiastic about Decorah is like announcing you hate puppies and kittens. Everybody loves Decorah. But for me, the town has conjured a complex mix of emotions.

Lutheranism was part of that same stewpot, because for years I equated it with conformity, a grim sense of duty, and judgmentalism. Even though I realized this wasn't fair—I knew many admirable Lutherans growing up—I still persisted in this estimation.

It didn't help that I had an unfortunate encounter with a Lutheran pastor at a surprise party for my mother's seventieth birthday at her church in Decorah. When the pastor asked how we'd gotten my mother into the building without letting her know about the party, I told her that I'd made up a story about a friend having an art exhibit there that I wanted her to see.

"You mean you lied to your mother," the pastor said.

When I laughed, assuming she was joking, she gave me a stern look, and though it had been many years since I was in Sunday School, I felt an immediate, Pavlovian response of guilt. This emotion was a familiar part of my childhood, because there were many ways one could fail in attempting to lead a good Lutheran life. I'd done so once again.

❧

Several years after that encounter, I finally began to reconsider my views on Decorah and Lutheranism after a seemingly ordinary event. My husband, Bob, had organized a volunteer day at a local park in our home of Iowa City, and a large group of Lutherans ranging from kids to the elderly signed up to work.

And did they work! Everybody knew how to use tools. They hacked, chainsawed, hoed, and clipped. Despite the chilly day, even the old guys were sweating. The group got through their tasks so quickly that Bob had to scramble to find enough activities to occupy them.

As Bob told me this story after he returned home, I couldn't help but contrast the energy and efficiency of the Lutherans to members of my own denomination, which by that time was the Episcopal Church. In a similar volunteer situation, I knew the group would have been much smaller. Of those who did sign up, several of us would cancel that morning. At least one person would write a long email explaining that she was passionately interested in the environment but something more important had come up that day. Of the remaining volunteers, most of us wouldn't know how to use a lopper, let alone a chainsaw. We'd talk at great length as we leaned against shovels and rakes, however, about the importance of having people get their hands dirty in nature. We'd have a lively discussion about how the parks department could better manage the property. And several of us would leave early because we had dinner reservations.

The Lutherans, meanwhile, would be starting on an extra set of tasks because they had all these hands and they may as well make the most of their time and are you sure we couldn't pull some of that invasive garlic mustard as long as we're here?

I was thoroughly Episcopalian in my preference for discussions instead of physical labor, but the contrast got me thinking.

Martin and Me, Reluctantly Reunited

It took a trip to Germany to help me fully understand what I'd experienced in my hometown all those years ago—and teach me how visits to holy sites can help us make sense of our personal histories in unexpected ways.

I wasn't particularly excited about touring Martin Luther sites in the former East Germany, but it was an option at a travel writing conference I attended, and as someone who specializes in spiritual tourism, I felt obliged to sign up. Filling out the online form, I reluctantly passed over the boxes for a cruise on the Danube, a hiking trek through Bavaria, and three days at Munich's Oktoberfest, instead checking "Martin Luther History" with a sigh.

When I arrived in Germany, however, I resolved to make the best of it. Our trip began in Wittenberg, the city most identified with Martin Luther and Reformation history. A guide dressed in the full-length skirt, hat, and cape of a sixteenth-century hausfrau met our small group of writers in the historic town center and gave us an overview of Luther's time in her city. Luther lived here for nearly 35 years, she said, first earning a doctorate in theology and then serving as a professor of Bible studies at the University of Wittenberg. She told us the story of how after he left the Roman Catholic Church he married Katharina von Bora, a former nun who'd escaped from her convent in an empty fish barrel and who was as strong-minded and formidable as her husband.

I was surprised to hear it was a happy union, for Martin Luther never struck me as good husband material, what with all his railing against corruption and preoccupation with sin, not to mention his notorious intestinal gas. But I learned that Luther loved his energetic, intelligent wife, referring to her as "my kind and dear lord and master, Katy, Lutheress, doctoress, and priestess of Wittenberg."

Our tour of Wittenberg continued, leading us to the house where the Luthers lived, now the world's largest museum of Reformation history, and St. Mary's Town Church, which is famous for its Reformation-era altar created by artist Lucas Cranach the Elder in 1547. We spent an entertaining hour in a print shop furnished as it would have been in Luther's day, its interior redolent with the sharp, chemical smell of ink. An artisan wearing a leather apron and period dress helped us print a sample page of a pamphlet, explaining how Wittenberg had been a center for publishing in the sixteenth century, which helped Luther's ideas spread quickly throughout Europe.

At last we came to the Castle Church, the site of the most famous bulletin board announcement in history. Our guide explained that in Luther's day, this church was the chapel for the university, and its side door functioned as a message board for church and school notices. Tradition says that on October 31, 1517, Luther walked up to that door and nailed on it a document, the 95 Theses, calling for reform in the Roman Catholic Church—an act that is credited with igniting the Protestant Reformation.

Though a fire destroyed the original door in 1760, a black bronze door now marks its location. Today pilgrims come from around the world to this spot. And standing in front of that door, my tepid interest in Martin Luther became genuine curiosity. Luther changed from the bronze statue I remembered from the Luther College campus—portly, stiff, and dull—into a living man.

Over the next three days, my interest grew as we followed the Martin Luther trail to Eisleben, the city of both his birth and death, and Erfurt, where he lived as a young man. As I traipsed from one historic site to another, I enjoyed the intellectual challenge of trying to make sense of the contradictory puzzle pieces of his life. He was a devout monk who became a loving husband, a committed Catholic who shattered the unity of the Church he loved, and an intellectual who didn't hesitate to use crude language to get his points across (for examples, see the online "Martin Luther Insult Generator").

Luther was the son of a miner who had become a prosperous copper smelter, a father who hoped his intelligent eldest son would raise the family's social standing by becoming a lawyer. Luther was a dutiful son and began his legal studies at the University of Erfurt. But on a summer night in 1505 he got caught in a terrible thunderstorm. Fearful for his life, he vowed to St. Anna that if he survived he would become a monk. When the danger passed, Luther kept his word by joining an Augustinian monastery in Erfurt, provoking the fury of his father.

In the monastery, Luther out-monked even the most zealous of his brothers. He was determined to save his soul through rigid discipline and penitence.

In 1511 he went to Rome. This wasn't a good year for idealistic monks to visit the Holy City, as the Church was in the middle of building St. Peter's Basilica and needed to raise a lot of money, fast. The selling of indulgences—which were said to release a soul from purgatory—was the primary means of filling the coffers. Luther was also appalled by the power, wealth, and corruption of the church hierarchy.

Returning to Germany, Luther struggled as well with the role of the Church in salvation, finally finding his answer in Paul's *Letter to the Romans* in the New Testament. Through Paul's words he came to believe that we are justified by faith, not works. No one can reach heaven through individual merit, because God alone can save sinners.

Luther launched a campaign to reform the Roman Catholic Church, which included nailing the theses on the church door in Wittenberg. He didn't intend to start a new branch of Christianity, but when the bishops and Pope Leo X opposed him, he turned on his former superiors with vehemence. After the pope threatened to excommunicate him if he didn't recant, Luther publicly burned the paper on which the threat was written, an in-your-face act not unlike young men burning their draft cards during the Vietnam War. The pope carried through on his threat, declaring Luther a pariah banned from participating in any Christian sacraments, thus putting his soul at risk of eternal damnation.

Then came Luther's finest moment. It took place in the German town of Worms at an assembly known as the Diet of Worms (a name that has delighted many generations of Lutheran children).

Any of us would be lucky to get something like this on our spiritual resumes, as it was quite riveting. Luther was brought before Charles V, the Holy Roman Emperor, to defend himself. Charles gave Luther the chance to renounce what he had preached and published. Luther stood up and said: "I cannot and I will not recant anything, for to go against conscience is neither right nor safe. God help me. Amen."

This statement, I had to admit, took *cojones* (an analogy that Luther probably would have liked). Luther affirmed the right of each person to claim a direct relationship with God. He stood up bravely to corruption and the threat of violence. He claimed the primacy of individual conscience over ecclesiastical hierarchy. It made me proud to be born a Lutheran, something I hadn't felt in many years.

Our last stop was Wartburg Castle, where Luther went into hiding after his act of defiance at the tribunal. A German prince who supported Luther's efforts for reform brought him to this fortress overlooking the town of Eisenach. Because there was a reward offered for his capture, Luther took off his monk's robe, grew a beard and long hair, and lived under an assumed name during his ten-month stay at the castle.

Our tour wound through the building's grand halls and richly ornamented public spaces. But its most famous room is much simpler and smaller, a space with rough-hewn walls and little furniture. It was here that Luther committed yet another revolutionary act, the translation of the New Testament into German. In its own way, this was even more provocative than his 95 Theses or his refusal to recant before the tribunal, because at that time church authorities strongly discouraged the translation of scripture into vernacular languages. This meant that knowledge of the Bible was largely limited to clergy. Luther, however, believed that all people had the right to read the divine word without ecclesiastical intermediaries.

Through the years I've learned that for me, the iron-clad test of whether I'm in a holy place is if my eyes well with tears. Unexpectedly, that happened in this humble room. For many years I'd disliked Martin Luther—he'd long struck me as grumpy, intolerant, and way too adamant about having me memorize his entire *Small Catechism*. But standing before his desk, I came to appreciate his courage and brilliance. His months of scribbling away in this drafty, chilly room changed the course of history, inspiring generations of Protestant Reformers as well as Johann Sebastian Bach, who tried to express in music what Luther penned in his theological writings. Luther's efforts contributed to the collapse of medieval feudalism and helped lay the foundation for the modern ideals of liberty and freedom of conscience.

Seeing his desk made me think, too, how many of the most powerful writings in history have been composed in prison or during exile, from the biblical book of Revelation written by a persecuted Christian on the island of Patmos to the "Letter from the Birmingham Jail" written by Luther's namesake, Martin Luther King, Jr. While authorities think that such forced isolation will silence and intimidate rebels, for some it deepens their commitment to justice and hardens their resolve. Alone with their thoughts and with God, countless prisoners of conscience have found their cells to be crucibles that temper and strengthen them.

As I left Luther's room, I saw a long line of people waiting to enter. With their earnest and reverent faces, they had the look of pilgrims, not merely tourists.

It's really quite amazing. One day you're an outlaw fearing for your life. And five centuries later, people from around the world come to pay homage to you in the room where you once sat writing at a desk.

Wayfaring with a Purpose

My time in Germany made me realize the foolishness of letting my childhood experiences define an entire faith. I'd been among the legions of people who think they understand their religious heritage despite studying it haphazardly during years when adolescent hormones bathed their brains and clouded their judgment. This is like thinking we've mastered particle physics because we managed to get a C in beginning algebra in junior high.

Germany also taught me about the power of pilgrimage to explain my past. I could see the direct connections between Luther's history and my own childhood in Iowa. Northern European industriousness helped shaped the work ethic of my small town. Even after centuries, Luther's persecution by the established church fueled the peculiar attitudes many Lutherans had towards Catholicism in my youth. And Luther's emphasis on the importance of an individual's relationship with God meant there was often more than a hint of Germanic angst in the air. You couldn't ride on anyone's coattails to heaven. Religion is serious stuff, and if you get it wrong you'll pay the price for eternity.

I probably didn't need to go all the way to Germany to learn these truths. But being right there where Luther nailed the 95 Theses to the church door and where he'd translated the New Testament made me understand these things in a way that I hadn't before.

But I must admit that in the end, my trip also confirmed for me why I'm no longer a Lutheran.

On my last day in Wittenberg, I attended a late afternoon, English-language service in a small stone chapel next to the Town Church. The liturgy was lovely, with a rousing rendition of the most famous Lutheran hymn of all, "A Mighty Fortress Is Our God." The song took me back to sitting in a pew at our country church and hearing the hymn played on its wheezy organ on Sunday mornings. I thought of my many relatives buried in its cemetery amid the Dahlens, Andersons, Halvorsons, Olsons, Johnsons, and Rosendahls, all of them enjoying the well-deserved eternal rest of Lutherans who've done their duty.

After the service ended, I sat for awhile in the church, alone. I reflected on what my time as a Lutheran had given me: a religious education steeped in the Bible, a no-nonsense, get-'er-done attitude towards volunteer service, and quite a few Bible verses that I still remembered from confirmation class, lo these many years ago. I hadn't ever been captured by the North Vietnamese, but I was still grateful to have them.

But as I sat there, the interior of the church became increasingly chilly and I got colder and colder. And it became a pretty apt metaphor for my relations with the Lutheran Church. This denomination is admirable. It is strong. If civilized society collapses in some sort of apocalyptic firestorm, I'm going to ditch the Episcopalians and try to find a band of roaming Lutherans, who will have re-created a fully functional society within 48 hours.

But until that day, I knew that Lutheranism would never be my faith again. For me it was too tied to ethnic identity, too steeped in a small town ethos, and too intertwined with memories of growing up. Some people find the faith of their childhood to be their anchor as adults, but that wasn't the case for me, even after I'd made my peace with Martin Luther.

By the time I left that little church, I was chilled to the bone.

Statue at Viking World in Reykjanesbær, Iceland

CHAPTER 2

DRAWING DOWN THE MOON

Any act based on love and pleasure is a ritual of the Goddess.
Her worship can take any form and occur anywhere; it
requires no liturgy, no cathedrals, no confessions.

Starhawk

~ PILGRIMAGE ~
On the Trail of Elves in Iceland

It's theoretically possible that I could have chosen someone more scandalous to get involved with than the Most Famous Goat Farmer in America, but it's a stretch to think who that might have been, at least within the confines of my small Iowa town.

I'd graduated in the spring from Luther and begun graduate school in English at the University of Iowa. On Labor Day weekend I was back in Decorah for a visit, and on that Saturday night I went to a dance at a former two-room schoolhouse in the countryside, a place where local folk musicians gathered to play once a month for a crowd of farmers, townsfolk, and college students. I'd loved going to the Highlandville Dances before I left Decorah, and I was pleased to be back.

It was a hot and humid night, unseasonably warm for late summer. I entered the room and looked across the floor, past all the couples spinning to the fiddle music, and there I saw a man I knew a little through mutual friends, but quite well by reputation. And that reputation wasn't good.

In Decorah, Bob was infamous. He hadn't embezzled money or been convicted of a crime, but he'd done something equally serious: he'd challenged the status quo of the local community. He and his wife had engaged in a high-profile legal fight for the right to home-school their three kids during an era when that was seen as truancy by the school authorities. The case attracted national attention, and Bob and his family were featured in media outlets that included *The New York Times* and *Phil Donahue Show*. Newspapers were fond of using a picture that showed a shaggy-haired Bob in his barn next to a goat, looking intense and intellectual as he adjusted the milking machine on her udder. He was, for a time, the Most Famous Goat Farmer in America.

All of the drama was chronicled in exhaustive detail by the Decorah newspaper, so everyone in town knew Bob. Some agreed with his crusade, but a lot of people tut-tutted. Why weren't the schools in Decorah good enough for those kids? And who was this radical who drew so much attention?

I knew that Bob and his wife had recently gotten a divorce, news that was greeted with a certain amount of satisfaction by many in town. He did indeed look like a man who'd gotten his proper comeuppance. During the past six months, in fact, he'd experienced a perfect trifecta of misery, having lost his wife, his farm, and his job working for a federal program helping underprivileged people find jobs (work he did in addition to goat farming, which wasn't lucrative enough to support a family). I saw him sitting alone in a corner, and I thought to myself, that's the saddest-looking man I've ever seen.

So I went over and asked him to dance.

For the next two years, I didn't think about anything other than Bob. Oh, I went back to Iowa City and attended classes, and I suppose I carried on my normal routine in many ways. But mainly what I did was have a passionate, whirlwind romance with the most interesting man I'd ever dated (though to be honest, that wasn't a very large pool).

Bob had a PhD in philosophy, was 16 years older than me, and had a past that included being a conscientious objector during Vietnam and stints as a college professor. This relationship clearly wasn't going to last, but I intended to enjoy myself while it did. After polishing my reputation as a Good Girl for years, I found to my surprise that when I wanted something as badly as I wanted Bob, I didn't care that much if it got tarnished a little.

All of this came as a surprise to my parents. For small town residents who'd always worried about what people thought, it was an awful thing to have people actually thinking about them. Bob was an undeniably poor choice of boyfriend—older than me, in debt, out of work, with three kids and no immediate prospects for improvement. My parents refused to meet him for a year, hoping he would just go away.

To say those next years were tempestuous would be an understatement, given the arguments with my family, financial stresses, issues relating to Bob's kids, and the challenges of being with someone still recovering from a hard divorce. Hardly a single person who knew us in those early days would have predicted our eventual happy marriage. But our bond grew deeper and stronger no matter what our external circumstances. Bob, notorious outlaw that he was, made me happy. And he thought I was an angel. We were surprisingly well-matched.

Many years later, when I was being ordained as a deacon in the Episcopal Church, I heard a story from our neighbor that's amused me ever since. Her daughter, who'd rarely attended a church service, misheard all the references to God and thought instead that the entire ordination service had the reverential, repeated refrain, "Thanks be to Bob."

So let me just echo that now: Thanks be to Bob. For the purposes of this spiritual tale, this contemporary spin on St. Augustine's *Confessions*, he's going to play a supporting role. But the foundation of this narrative, and of my entire life, is his love and devotion, no matter what deity I happened to be dating.

Playing with the Pagans

After two years of thinking only about Bob, I eventually had some attention left over for other matters. By this time both of us had undergone some changes. Bob was teaching at a community college, becoming less *Mother Earth News* and more *Chronicle of Higher Education*, with a better haircut and no facial hair. I'd left graduate school with an MA in English after growing bored with academia on the path to a PhD. Unprepared for anything practical, I started freelance writing, which despite its uncertainties suited me because I love being my own boss. We lived in the university town of Iowa City, a lively community with a much broader range of people and cultural opportunities than I'd encountered before.

During this period in my mid-20s, I became more interested in spirituality, in part through conversations with friends who had different religious backgrounds than mine and also by reading my way through the religion section of the public library. The more I learned, the more fascinated I became by what a big, colorful, rowdy circus it is. There's Hinduism and Sufism and Orthodox Judaism, Rastafarians who worship a Black Jesus and the Amish who eschew electricity, followers of Santeria who sacrifice chickens and Jains who try to avoid killing even the smallest of creatures. Folks out there were using peyote, speaking in tongues, handling snakes, going on vision quests, and performing a multitude of other profoundly non-Lutheran activities.

Of the array of religions, the one that most appealed to me was Wicca. A variety of neo-paganism, Wicca began to attract national attention in the 1980s, culminating in its recognition as a legitimate religion by the U.S. government in 1986. Among its best-known practitioners during this era was NPR reporter Margot Adler, author of *Drawing Down the Moon: Witches, Druids, Goddess-Worshippers, and Other Pagans in America.* From her I learned that Wicca has nothing to do with Satanism or black magic, but instead celebrates the natural world and the sacredness of all living things. While it draws on ancient traditions, particularly shamanism, Wicca was reborn and reconstituted in the twentieth century by people who wanted an earth-based spirituality unencumbered by what they saw as the patriarchal structure of Western religions. Many of its practitioners have reclaimed the term *witch*, which simply means a follower of Wicca.

Bob, who'd been raised a Methodist but hadn't practiced any religion for years, wasn't fazed when his Lutheran-farmer's-daughter girlfriend became a witch, though he did ask me not to tell his parents about it (I didn't tell mine either, figuring that I'd shocked them enough). I was an enthusiastic convert, attending workshops and retreats that I learned about through the bulletin board at the local food co-op, devouring books in the Women's Spirituality section of the library, and assembling my Wiccan tool kit of candles, crystals, chalice, and bell. I bought a lunar calendar and celebrated the solstices, equinoxes, and the pagan Celtic holidays. I learned how to read tarot cards—not the creepy, older versions of the tarot, but instead a feminist deck with multi-ethnic, full-bodied earth mothers, maidens, and crones, as well as a few spindly-looking men.

Not for the last time, books became my primary spiritual practice, from Merlin Stone's *When God Was a Woman* to Monica Sjoo's *The Great Cosmic Mother*. Of the many that I read, the most influential was *The Spiral Dance: A Rebirth of the Ancient Religion of the Great Goddess* by the lyrically named Starhawk. In it she writes that Wicca is a religion of poetry, not theology. I was especially taken by her explanation that Wicca has no concept of sin, in contrast to what I'd learned from Luther in his *Small Catechism*:

> *What have you deserved from God because of your sins?*
> His wrath and displeasure, temporal death, and eternal damnation.

Instead, the Wiccans had this cheery principle: "What you send, returns to you three times over." If we send out love, it will return to us multiplied. If we send negativity and anger, ditto. I liked how simple and straightforward it was.

From a Wiccan perspective, magic—which is defined as the art of sensing and shaping the subtle, unseen forces that flow through the world—is not something just for fairy tales. You could cast a spell to heal a broken heart, win in court, or dispel loneliness. You didn't need a church or a minister, either, but instead could create sacred space anywhere with intention and a candle. I tried my hand at casting some spells myself (to attract money; they didn't work). Looking back now, I realize this process has a lot in common with prayer, as both activities help us slow down, focus, and connect with the inner promptings of our hearts.

Until Starhawk and other authors pointed it out to me, I hadn't realized how steeped in masculine images Christianity is. There's God the

Father, of course, but also all the references to men in the fine print. I decided that I'd had enough of a male god, leaving him behind not so much out of resentment, but rather because it was so intriguing to think of the divine in feminine terms.

In my search for a replacement, I learned about dozens of goddesses, from Brigid and Cerridwen in the Celtic tradition to Artemis in the Greek and Freyja in the Norse. After some deliberation I decided to go more universal, transferring my allegiance simply to the Goddess, a divine being whose energy flowed through all of creation. She wasn't just God in a dress, but rather a metaphor that infused the entire world with divinity. In the words of Starhawk: "The Goddess is not separate from the world—She *is* the world, and all things in it: moon, sun, earth, star, stone, seed, flowing river, wind, wave, leaf and branch, bud and blossom, fang and claw, woman and man."

I remembered that the woods on our farm had always felt alive with more than just trees, birds, and squirrels. As a girl I believed there might be a portal within the forest to some other dimension, and if I could just find it I would enter into a magical place that was like our farm but different, like when Dorothy reaches Oz and brilliant colors flood her black-and-white world. Playing around with spells and rituals took me back to those days, making me feel childlike in the best sense of the word.

I especially loved being tied to the lunar cycle. I didn't need to do much in terms of ritual, for just standing in our backyard on warm nights under a full moon was enough. Bathed in its silvery light, I gazed upward and imagined its energy flowing into me. With the night air caressing my skin, the hum and rasp of insects and the hooting of the occasional owl, it was more meaningful than any church service I'd ever attended.

"Every full moon has a name, from the Wolf Moon of January to the Long Night Moon of December," a retreat leader told me. "Every phase of the moon has meaning, too. A waxing moon is a time for growth and new projects, and a waning one a time to get rid of old habits or bad energy. People have been following the cycles of the moon for millennia. There's deep wisdom to be found in meditating on the moon."

Part of what I felt on those nights was a sense of connection to the spiritual seekers of the past, those who for countless generations looked up at the night sky, studied the stars, and spun stories around campfires. I suspect this was how a longing for transcendence began in our species, not in the harsh light of day but in darkness pierced by stars and lit by the soft glow of the moon, serenaded by our fellow creatures, who sang to us in words we couldn't understand.

Parts of Wicca were a little dubious to me, I must admit. I didn't buy the theory that before Judeo-Christian cultures appeared on the scene, Goddess-worshipping peoples were all peaceful, harmonious societies. I'd studied enough anthropology to realize that back in the good-ole days When God Was A Woman, sometimes all that would keep her happy was human sacrifice.

It was hard to sustain a community of like-minded practitioners, too, for the connections I made at workshops didn't last very long. People would finish up their graduate degrees and leave town or discover they were actually more Buddhist than Wiccan. Or they'd move to nearby Fairfield to attend the Maharishi University of Management, where the students meditate twice a day under two golden domes, one for men and one for women. (Yes, the school's in Iowa. It's a long story.)

But for several years I remained a Wiccan, content to take the bad with the good. I'd done the same with Lutheranism, after all.

❧

In the end, I left Wicca not with a bang, but a whimper. It wasn't that I became disillusioned or had conflicts with other believers or got struck by lightning while standing on a hill at Samhain (the Celtic holiday on which Halloween is based). It's just that it's hard to keep a religion going when you're doing most of it by yourself. I'd read so many books on Wicca that they all started to run together. My deck of tarot cards was pushed to the back of a drawer and largely forgotten. The summer solstice came and went and I didn't even notice.

I'd become a lapsed witch.

Years later when I first heard the derivation of the word *religion*, I understood what happened to me. Religion comes from the Latin *ligare*, meaning "to bind." That gets to the heart of what religion is about: the precepts and rituals that bind communities and generations together. Followers of a faith often chafe at the rules. We rebel and wrestle with doctrines and complain. But there's a structure deeply embedded in a religion that keeps the tradition alive even when its individual members falter. During my Wiccan years, I was spiritual but not religious, and that's a hard path to sustain for very long, especially when so many bright and shiny objects were distracting me along the way.

But looking back on my time as a neo-pagan, I'm grateful for what I learned. To this day I believe that what I send out into the world comes back to me magnified. I wish I could say I try to refrain from malice because of some higher moral standard, but instead it's probably more due to this belief left over from my Wiccan days. And here's a corollary: I think hate can create a psychic tie between us and those we despise, keeping us linked in a grim union of perpetual resentment. That cautionary commandment has served me well over the years, too.

From Wicca I also gained a lasting appreciation for the importance of imagination and creativity in spirituality. In my childhood, religion was given to me fully formed. You could take it or leave it, but you couldn't play with it. Wicca allowed me to tap back into a primal sense that the world is suffused with wonders. If we just pay attention, even a sunset should bring us to our knees.

And even though it's been many years since I was on Team Goddess, I'm still enthralled by the moon. On the nights when it's full I'll stand outside and watch as it rises above the rooftops, binding me to something ancient that can't be expressed in words, only felt as a faint but unmistakable shiver of mystery.

With the Dirty Children of Eve in Iceland

My time as a Wiccan taught me about the difficulty of re-constructing a religious tradition once it's largely been abandoned. But on my travels I discovered a place where people are bringing back that Old Time Religion more successfully—Iceland, land of fire and snow, volcanoes and glaciers, Thor and Freya, and the Hidden People, a.k.a. elves.

Over the past century, a large percentage of Icelanders experienced the same sort of falling out with Lutheranism that I did in my younger years. While many Icelanders believe in God, only a small fraction go to church more than once or twice a year. Instead, they have a spiritual connection to the land and to the pre-Christian myths and stories of their nation. For them, an earth-based spirituality is a living faith.

My trip to Iceland became a pilgrimage for me in part because of its connection to Norway, the country from which my great-grandparents emigrated. The Norwegians came to Iceland in the ninth century, colonizing a land that was unoccupied except for a few Irish monks, who left in a hurry once the Vikings arrived, having seen what sort of houseguests they'd been in Ireland. My ancestor, the famous explorer Leif Eriksson, was born in Iceland of Norwegian stock and became the first European to visit North America around the year 1000. In the capital of Reykjavik is a statue of him atop a tall spire, looking noble and handsome, a man anyone would be happy to have in the family gene pool.

My first order of business was to have Bob take a picture of me with my illustrious forefather (though genealogical research hasn't proved it yet, I know we must be related because we share a sense of wanderlust and a last name). Next we hit the open road—or more specifically, the Ring Road, the 830-mile highway that winds along the coastline of the main island of Iceland.

As we drove, we kept comparing the landscape to other places we'd been, from Scotland and New Zealand to Wyoming. But gradually we fell silent, for the ever-changing vistas were unlike anything we'd experienced before. Iceland has a blend of landscapes so diverse it's as if God used the island as a petri dish of geologic experimentation. The countryside is both gorgeously green and as bleak as the surface of the moon, with cold winds that chill you and bubbling geothermal pools that warm you back up again. It holds mountains, waterfalls, tundra, high deserts, and lush pastures. Other than one 15-minute nap, I don't think I missed a single second of the entire eight-day trip. I was enthralled by what was unfolding, and each night I dreamed of what we had seen that day, the images and colors gliding one into the next with wraith-like fluidity.

Elves became a theme of our trip beginning on the first day. After eating dinner in the hotel's restaurant, we browsed the adjacent gift shop. As I peered at the assortment of elf figurines for sale on its shelves, trying to decide which bearded imp to purchase, a clerk came over to chat.

"We have a lot of elves in Iceland, you know," she said, looking entirely normal despite what she had just said. "More than half of us believe in the Hidden People."

When I asked if she herself had ever seen one, she assured me she had. "Go up to the park on the edge of town early in the morning and you might see some yourself," she said.

One of the things I love about Bob is that when I suggest we get up early to hunt for elves, he doesn't say no, but instead asks what time we need to leave. So the next morning we set off into the woods, walking slowly as we peered underneath bushes and listened intently for unusual noises. Occasionally I'd announce, "Boy, it sure would be nice to see some elves."

In my line of work this is called *research*.

We did a lot of elf research in Iceland. Before arriving, I'd read stories of how a significant percentage of Icelanders at least entertain the possibility of elves, and that road planners have been known to avoid places said to be home to *Huldufólk,* or Hidden People. In my Norwegian-marinated hometown, *nisse* are merely cute window decorations, but in Iceland supernatural beings are seen as occasionally cantankerous but generally good neighbors, provided they're treated with respect.

I asked a wide range of Icelanders their opinions of Hidden People, from tour guides and college professors to locals we met while soaking in the geothermal hot tubs that are a major part of Icelandic social life. Their responses had a surprising amount of unanimity. While few had actually seen one of these creatures themselves, virtually everyone had an open mind about their existence. The only person who flat-out denied the possibility of elves was a geologist who worked at one of the national parks (note to self: do not try again to interview scientists about magical creatures).

Several Icelanders related the story of why the Hidden People are sometimes called the "Dirty Children of Eve." When God asked Eve to introduce him to her children, she only had time to clean some of them up. So she hid the rest, and they've stayed hidden ever since.

Other people told stories of how the Hidden People wear elegant clothes, typically in the styles of an earlier age. These beings have more in common with the elves of J.R.R. Tolkien's *Lord of the Rings* than the leprechauns of Ireland (in fact, Tolkien was deeply influenced by Icelandic stories). "My grandmother saw them in a meadow once, and they were dressed in fancy outfits," a man said. "She was a militant atheist when it came to religious matters, but to her dying day she believed in elves."

As we traveled, I was struck by how my perceptions of the landscape changed because of my search for the Hidden People. I walked more slowly and attentively on our Icelandic hikes than I ever had before, inspecting clusters of stones and clumps of bushes as we passed, peering into their shadows for a telltale shimmer or a glimpse of finery. Call me naive, but that half-playful, half-serious perspective greatly deepened my appreciation of Iceland.

Most of us live in a disenchanted world, but in Iceland nature is so raw and immediate that magic seems possible. In a land of volcanoes, earthquakes, swirling Northern Lights, and nearly constant wind, you know that you're small and insignificant and that the earth has more powers in it than you can understand. Including, perhaps, the Hidden People.

Paging Thor and Odin

While many Icelanders believe elves might inhabit their country, a significant subset goes a step further and thinks that the Old Norse gods and goddesses might be hanging around, too.

Hilmar Örn Hilmarsson believes they are. Hilmar is a well-known musician, film composer, and art director in Iceland. But I talked to him because of another role he plays: *allsherjargoði*, or chief priest, of the religion Ásatrú, the revived faith in the Old Norse pantheon. On a gray morning in Reykjavik at the end of our Ring Road tour, we spoke

31

about Iceland's history, its holy places, and what it takes to bring a dormant religion back to life.

We met in the nondescript storefront that is the headquarters for Ásatrú (though a new temple is being constructed to the Old Norse gods near Reykjavik, the first to be built in Iceland in a thousand years). Sporting a neatly trimmed beard and wearing a wool sweater with the intricately stitched yoke that is practically a uniform among Icelanders, Hilmar had kind eyes and a soft-spoken manner. He struck me as someone who has done his spiritual homework.

He began by sketching a brief history of how Christianity came to be adopted in Iceland in the year 1000. "There was huge political and economic pressure from the other Nordic countries to convert," he said. "But even after Iceland became officially Christian, many people continued to follow the older traditions for a time."

After that, the stories of Odin, Thor, Freyja and their divine kindred were primarily kept alive in the literature of Iceland, particularly in the collections of Old Norse myths and stories known as *The Poetic Edda* and *The Prose Edda*. Under the guise of reading literature, people learned about their pagan heritage.

The roots of the modern revival of the religion date back to the nineteenth century. The Romantic Movement in Europe included a fascination with Old Norse culture, while in Iceland a revitalized sense of national identity looked to the past for inspiration. A century later, a small group of Icelanders came together to found Ásatrú, a word meaning "belief in the gods" in Old Norse. In 1973 the Icelandic government recognized it as an official religion, with legal authority to conduct weddings and burials. It has holidays, including the winter and summer solstices, the first day of summer, and a mid-winter celebration called Thorrablot, which honors the god Thor. While Ásatrú has no sacred text, its precepts include tolerance, honesty, honor, and respect for the cultural heritage and natural world of Iceland.

Hilmar has had a ringside seat for the revival of Ásatrú: when he joined the community at the age of 16, he was number 36 on its official registry. He said that in its first decades the religion remained small and was viewed skeptically by many Icelanders, but eventually public opinion changed. "Slowly people began to see we were serious," Hilmar said. "Today there's considerable interest in what we do even if people aren't official members. About 40 percent of Icelanders describe their religious viewpoint as pagan. I'm happy to say that our relations with Christian leaders have improved as well. There's a sense of mutual respect between us."

Here's what I liked best about what he said during our time together, something that reminded me of what had so appealed to me about Wicca in the past: "Fundamentally, we're a nature-based religion," said Hilmar. "In Iceland, we're humbled by nature every day. The land is active. You can sense it beneath your feet. It's easy to feel awe here."

The question of whether an ancient Norse warrior would recognize the rituals of the religion gets to the heart of the challenges of reviving a faith, whether it's Wicca or Ásatrú. Because the culture of Iceland has changed so dramatically (no more chieftains fiercely guarding their honor or long boats setting off for foreign shores), simply copying the practices of a former era is not possible. How can a person believe in Thor as a thunder-maker while knowing the physics of lightning? But I think Ásatrú is saving the best parts of the old traditions: a deep respect for the natural world, a sense that there are powers far beyond human understanding, and an appreciation for the myths and stories that shaped the Icelandic world for centuries. And like any good religion,

Ásatrú provides community for its followers and a guide for navigating the transitions of birth, marriage, and death.

The Icelanders have deep pagan roots, and today as Christianity wanes in much of Western Europe, these older traditions are resurfacing—similar to the volcanoes that periodically come back to life from under the glaciers in Iceland.

⁕

Holy sites in Iceland are somewhat of a misnomer, for many people consider all of its landscape to be spiritually alive. But Hilmar identified two spots that we'd been fortunate to visit on our trip on the Ring Road.

Thingvellir is the most significant, the "spiritual and symbolic heart of Iceland," according to Hilmar. Now a national park, it sits on the fault line between the Eurasian and North American tectonic plates that are moving apart at the pace of about an inch a year. Because this fault line is hidden under the ocean everywhere else, this is the one spot it can be easily viewed; the only other place in the world to observe two major tectonic plates separating is the Great Rift Valley of eastern Africa.

Thingvellir has broad plains, lava fields, low-lying mountains, a river with a picturesque waterfall, and a lake—sort of an Iceland in miniature. We visited it during a blustery rainstorm, which was inconvenient but certainly added to the drama of the place. The power in the air was palpable, and it wasn't just the wind and rain.

The Althing, an open-air assembly of representatives from all of Iceland, began meeting here in 930 and continued in an annual conclave for nearly nine centuries. Given the Icelanders' long experience with the unseen forces of their landscape, I suspect they knew that something simmers here. And in 1944 when Iceland declared its independence from Denmark, people came here, appropriately, to celebrate.

I was even more impressed by the sacred site of Helgafell, though on the surface it's less physically imposing than Thingvellir. Located on the north coast of the Snæfellsnes peninsula, Helgafell is mentioned in the *Sagas*, the stories of early Icelandic history. For centuries the promontory was a place of pilgrimage, particularly for those nearing death, as it was believed to be an entry point into the afterlife. It was said that from its peak, people could sometimes see Valhalla, the paradise of warriors.

Helgafell's sacred past lives on today in the belief that those who climb it for the first time will be granted three wishes, provided they follow these rules: As they ascend, they cannot look back; they must walk in silence; and they can never reveal their wishes to others.

I know that when Bob and I stood on the top of Helgafell after a half-hour climb, that windswept peak felt like many other holy sites we've visited––a thin place, as the ancient Celts would say, a spot where the boundary between worlds is transparent. Like countless pilgrims before, we'd followed the simple rules, which are likely a watered-down form of older and more complicated rituals. But enduring truths are embedded in those instructions: Dwelling on the past will get you nowhere. Silence is an essential spiritual discipline. And a wise seeker keeps her innermost thoughts private.

Perhaps it's because of my Scandinavian heritage, but for a few moments, looking at the landscape of misty mountains in the distance, opalescent water in the bay below, and a bank of clouds pierced by shafts of sunlight, I had no difficulty at all in believing that I was seeing Valhalla.

ᗡ

On our last day in Iceland, Bob and I took a guided hike across a glacier, carefully inching our way on icy surfaces past deep crevices. On our way back to the tour bus after the trek, we were relieved to be on firm footing once again as we walked through a lush valley carpeted with emerald green grass and moss.

Bob and the rest of the group had walked ahead, leaving me alone with our handsome young guide. I peppered him with questions about the Hidden People, for while I was resigned to the fact I wasn't going to see any elves in Iceland, I could at least gather a few final pieces of information about them.

As we walked, the young man answered my questions with great patience. Then he stopped to point out a large rock in the distance. "That's an elf church," he said. "I've never seen anything there, but some people have."

He told me of the many Icelandic stories of humans falling in love with elves. "Sometimes, you see, people don't realize they've met one of the Hidden People," he explained. "It's only after they've fallen in love that the truth is revealed, and then they have to decide whether they're going to go through the stones and join the elves forever."

When he mentioned that there's a folk song about just such a story, I asked if he could share it with me. After protesting that he didn't have a good voice, he started singing in a resonant, clear tenor.

As we walked down that verdant valley, he continued the song, the tune haunting and strange. I couldn't understand the words, but I knew they were filled with longing and sadness, and that the language I was hearing hadn't changed much since the Vikings had walked this same landscape.

It was, beyond a doubt, a magical interlude, one of my most cherished memories from Iceland. And looking back, I'm not entirely certain my guide was human.

Henry David Thoreau's grave in Concord, Massachusetts

CHAPTER 3

WRITING MY WAY AROUND THE WORLD

*All journeys have secret destinations of which
the traveler is unaware.*

Martin Buber

~ PILGRIMAGE ~
At Walden Pond in Concord, Massachusetts

S ometimes, holy places sneak up on us—and we don't have to travel far to find them, either, since every part of the world has places that exert a powerful pull on the human spirit.

I found this to be true on a family vacation to Massachusetts, where we enjoyed attractions ranging from whale-watching off Cape Ann to touring downtown Boston. But what I loved most was visiting Concord, a small town famous both as the site of the first battle of the American Revolution and as the center of a remarkable literary and philosophical community in the mid-nineteenth century.

Excitement mounted as we approached Concord, because in my family there's hardly anything more exciting than following in the footsteps of dead philosophers.

Let's say you could step into a time machine that would take you to 1840s Concord. You'd likely be impressed by Ralph Waldo Emerson, a tall, handsome man with a kindly manner, and by Louisa May Alcott's quick wit and intelligence. Brooding Nathaniel Hawthorne wouldn't talk much to you, but you could probably sense there was a great mind at work behind his shyness.

Then there's Henry David Thoreau, who would probably strike you as someone unlikely to amount to much.

Thoreau was born into a family that owned a small pencil-making factory and grew to be a short, thin, agile, and boyish man. Susan Cheever, whose fascinating book *American Bloomsbury* prepared me for our trip to Concord, writes that the only big things about Thoreau were his nose and his ideas.

With his wild hair and shabby clothes, Thoreau had little concern for his physical appearance and was more comfortable around children than adults. In addition to working in the family business, he was a surveyor, gardener, and skilled craftsman. Most of all, he loved the outdoors, spending large amounts of his time in the woods and paddling the waterways of the surrounding countryside.

"For many years I was self-appointed inspector of snow-storms and rain-storms," he wrote, "and did my duty faithfully, though I never received one cent for it."

In 1838, Thoreau opened a small school in Concord with his brother John, one that was attended by local children who included Louisa May Alcott and her sisters. Its methods were influenced by the educational ideas of Bronson Alcott, Louisa's father, and its classes featured nature study as well as standard courses such as mathematics and Latin.

I envy the pupils in Thoreau's classroom, for his knowledge of the natural world was so wide-ranging that it was deemed nearly magical by his students. Announcing in the morning his intention to take them on a visit to heaven that day, he would introduce them to wonders such as cobwebs spun between stalks of grass and fish lurking in the shallows of the river.

During Thoreau's lifetime, his own meager reputation as a writer was far overshadowed by that of his friend and mentor Emerson, who assisted him financially for years. Emerson gave Thoreau loans, found him work, and encouraged him in his writing. Their relationship was not without strains, as Emerson's assistance could shade over into paternalism, and at times Thoreau greatly resented being dependent upon him.

But in the story of their friendship, one act stands above all others: in 1845, Emerson gave Thoreau the use of some land he owned on the outskirts of Concord near Walden Pond.

Thoreau was 27 years old when he built his cabin on the shore of the lake, which is a small body of water a half-mile in length. The building of it must have been an intoxicating experience for him, this man who had so often relied on charity but who now was independent (though admittedly he was living rent-free on land belonging to a friend). He spent his days writing in his journal and working on the manuscript of what would become *A Week on the Concord and Merrimack Rivers.* He fished, played his flute, and tramped through the forest, keenly observing the changes of the seasons in the woods and waters around him.

His emotional life was troubled: his brother had died, his teaching career had floundered, and his prospects for a writing career looked bleak. He took solace not only in nature, but in the companionship of friends. He frequently walked into town to socialize, and entertained guests in his home as well.

While the popular image of him is of a recluse and loner, he actually enjoyed the companionship of like-minded folks. "I had three chairs in my house; one for solitude, two for friendship, three for society," he wrote in *Walden*, his book recalling his time living in the woods. "When visitors came in larger and unexpected numbers there was but the third chair for them all, but they generally economized the room by standing up. It is surprising how many great men and women a small house will contain."

After two years, he decided that his experiment in simple living had run its course, and he moved back into Concord. "I left the woods for as good a reason as I went there," he wrote. "Perhaps it seemed to me that I had several more lives to live, and could not spare any time for that one."

Thoreau spent seven years editing the journals he kept at the lake cabin. The result was *Walden*, a book that calls us to a new way of living, one of simplicity and harmony with the natural world. The prose is both down-to-earth (detailing the amount of money he spent on each part of his house, for example) and lyrical in its descriptions of the landscape around him. Its pages celebrate the joys of a life lived thoughtfully and deliberately.

Reading *Walden*, it's easy to miss the despair that underlies the writing of it. In *American Bloomsbury*, Susan Cheever speculates that part of why Thoreau was able to create his masterpiece is that he likely felt that he had nothing more to lose. Grieving his brother, realizing that he was never going to be a success in any conventional sense, he wrote with an honesty and passion not found in his other works.

Thoreau became sick soon after the publication of *Walden* in 1855. He had tuberculosis, and his lungs were further damaged by working amid the dust and lead shavings of his family's pencil factory. When someone asked him if he had made his peace with God, Thoreau replied, "I didn't know we had ever quarreled."

Concord, which for years had shaken its collective head at his peculiarities, realized that it loved him after all. At his death in 1862, the town's children were let out of school to attend his funeral and the church bells tolled 44 times, one for each year of his life. Appropriately, his coffin was covered with wildflowers.

Thoreau earned nothing from the publication of *Walden*, and at his death he was regarded as a minor disciple of Emerson, at best. But in the ensuing years his reputation and influence have grown: as with all prophets, the full worth of his words are only appreciated with the passage of time. His essay, "On the Duty of Civil Disobedience," written after he spent a night in the Concord jail for refusing to pay his taxes because of the country's support for slavery and the Mexican-American War, has had a profound influence on activists that include Gandhi and Martin Luther King, Jr. The philosophical movement he helped found, Transcendentalism, became the basis for much of the modern environmental movement and deeply shaped the course of American religious thought.

Transcendentalism, that multi-syllabled, amorphous word that is most associated with Thoreau and Emerson, was inspired in part by Eastern spiritual traditions. Thoreau and his friends believed that beneath the surface of everyday life is a deeper, more coherent reality that can be accessed only by intuition. Like many people in our time, members of this circle were spiritual-but-not-religious, with a focus on the individual rather than the communal. They believed that nature is a divine roadmap full of signs, and that if we follow its guidance we'll be able to comprehend both ourselves and the entire cosmos. While they knew very well the suffering and evils of human life, they rejected the doctrine of Original Sin espoused by the Calvinists and Puritans and thought that if people fulfilled their potential—that is, if they attained self-realization—much misery would disappear.

Of all Thoreau's writings, *Walden* speaks most clearly to people across the years, inspiring countless readers to march to the beat of a different drummer, to use Thoreau's phrase that has become a cliché simply because it is so apt. The writings of his contemporaries often strike contemporary ears as dated and antique, but many of Thoreau's words are as vivid and immediate as if they were being written today.

❧

Though I'd known quite a bit about Thoreau's life before visiting Concord, my tour of his hometown made me realize the extent of his influence on my own path—and that's the moment when the trip that I thought was a family vacation became a pilgrimage.

I'd first read *Walden* in a college class. I returned to the book a decade later, seeking answers on how to follow a path of voluntary simplicity in my own life. From Thoreau I learned that living small could paradoxically allow a person to live large, for voluntary simplicity opens up a wealth of opportunities, both practical and spiritual. Thoreau is one of the reasons why Bob and I live in a modest home and why we try to use things up, wear them out, make them do, or do without. Walking in his footsteps around Concord made me realize all the ways in which I'd walked in his footsteps in my own life.

By the time I stepped onto the path that leads to the spot in the woods where Thoreau's cabin once stood, I knew I was approaching sacred ground. It was a warm summer day, and with each step the noise of people's conversations in the parking lot became more muted and the sounds of the forest—the rustling of leaves, twitter of birds, and murmur of wind in the branches—became louder. I came into a clearing where posts mark the place Thoreau's cabin had been. Just down the hill I could see Walden Pond, ringed by thick woods, its surface sparkling with sunlight, looking very similar, most likely, to when Thoreau lived here.

Next to the site was a sign bearing these lines from *Walden*:

I went to the woods because I wished to live deliberately, to front only the essential facts of life, and see if I could not learn what it had to teach, and not, when I came to die, discover that I had not lived.

The words made me realize how much wisdom Thoreau had gained from remaining in one small town. "I have traveled a good deal in Concord," he wrote in *Walden*, honoring the insights he absorbed from walking its streets, visiting with his neighbors, and exploring the surrounding countryside. Thoreau's life is a reminder that not every pilgrimage involves packing a suitcase. Many seekers have experienced profound connections to the divine right where they live, and plenty of people who go on trips to the world's great holy sites end up complaining about the weather, the crowds, and the food. Pilgrimages are made by intention and grace, not by distance. Thoreau was a pilgrim each day of his life in Concord.

Pity the Poor Travel Writers

I'd already known of Thoreau's great influence on my philosophy of life. But my trip to Concord made me realize how much we had in common as freelance writers. Though he scribbled away with paper and pen and I tapped the keys on a computer, I suspect we both spent an inordinate amount of time staring into space as we struggled to find words. Hearing about the disappointing sales of *Walden* made me think of all the writing projects I'd started with high hopes only to see them end in disappointment.

And on a more prosaic note, like Thoreau I was occasionally mistaken for a bum.

Take the time I was on a *Mississippi Queen* cruise between New Orleans and Natchez, Mississippi. The trip itself was glorious, with bountiful food, shore tours of historic antebellum homes, and slowly changing river scenery that we viewed from our private balcony. On the last night, I got to sit next to the captain at dinner because it was my birthday. People sang in my honor and afterwards Bob and I danced in the moonlight on the top deck.

The next afternoon, after landing in New Orleans we headed to the rail station. To save money, we'd originally traveled by train rather than airplane to New Orleans, and on the overnight trip back we slept in our seats as best as we could, arriving bleary-eyed in Chicago the next morning. Before starting the next leg of our trip, we ate breakfast in a nearby restaurant, after which I went to find the bathroom.

I was standing in front of the mirror when I realized someone was staring at me: a smartly dressed businesswoman who had a look of disdain on her face. Mystified, I looked down at myself. I realized I was surrounded by bags. I'd clearly slept rough the night before. And I was brushing my teeth in the sink. She obviously thought I was a street person.

I stood there for a moment and considered telling her that two days ago I'd been sitting at the captain's table on the *Mississippi Queen*, but I realized she wouldn't believe me. I ran a hand over my disheveled hair, smiled weakly at her, and scurried out.

This story pretty much sums up what being a travel writer is like. It's all there—the incredible experiences, the V.I.P. attention, and then the abrupt shift back to reality when you're on your own dime and trying to be as frugal as possible because travel writing pays so little.

I occasionally get asked how I got into travel writing, often with some amount of envy. Who wouldn't want the opportunity to travel the world, be wined and dined in the finest restaurants, and be your own boss?

Let me tell you about the downsides of being a travel writer, though I realize that sympathy for my profession doesn't come easy. But here's the truth of it:

1. Just as some people have won hundreds of millions of dollars in a lottery, there are also travel writers with well-paying, secure jobs. The odds of both of these happening are similar.

2. With our sky-high-deductible health insurance policies, travel writers don't go to the doctor unless we need more than five stitches or have tried all treatments recommended by Dr. Google.

3. We're routinely forgotten by editors. They've never seen our faces. They have no personal connection to us. Their inboxes are full of over-eager freelancers clamoring for attention.

4. Rejections R Us. I estimate that I've been rejected more than 1,000 times in my 30-year writing career, sometimes politely, occasionally warmly, most often with no response at all. While it gets easier with time, it never totally loses its sting.

5. An inverse relationship exists between how much we're paid and the amount of enjoyment we take in the assignment. For a 2,000-word piece on ice festivals across the country, the payment is relatively generous. We'll attend none of these festivals, because we're writing the article in July. Instead we'll make several dozen phone calls to festival organizers, who can't tell us much about what their ice festival will include because it's, ahem, *July*. We'll labor to make the two-sentence descriptions of each of these festivals sound unique and appealing. We'll look up "ice" in the thesaurus to find ways to vary the text with synonyms. We won't find very many.

6. One of the worst days of the year is when we receive our estimate of future benefits from the Social Security Administration. We see what our net income has been for all the years we've been working. We look into the future and see our friends enjoying their last years in the palatial environs of the retirement community with the elegant dining room and on-staff massage therapist. Instead there's a good chance we'll be living in the spare bedroom of one of our children. We're extra nice to our offspring, hoping that one of them will take us in when we can no longer earn $200 for 600-word articles on the best fishing spots in Iowa.

It's a good thing Thoreau had Emerson, because every freelancer needs a wealthy—and generous—best friend.

❧

When Bob and I reminisce about travels we've taken, we have a long list of wonderful destinations to recall. At some point one of us will bring up the very first, the journey that set the standard for all other trips. "Do you remember *Indianapolis?*" Bob says, a faraway look in his eyes.

I'd become a travel writer somewhat by accident soon after I started freelancing. I was happy to write about anything as long as it resulted in a check, and I'd sent out hundreds of queries to magazines on topics ranging from how to set up a home office to a field guide to roadkill written by a biologist friend. A lucky break came when one of those queries resulted in an assignment from a national travel magazine for an article on farm vacations, the Midwestern equivalent of a dude ranch. I'd told the editor that while I wasn't a published writer, as a farmer's daughter I knew one end of a dairy cow from the other and so was uniquely qualified to write the piece. *Voilà!* I was a travel writer—for in the wild and wooly world of freelancing, chutzpah is as important as credentials.

That first assignment set the pattern of my work for a number of years. Especially when you're a newbie, most travel writing gigs aren't about romantic trips to Tuscany or African photo safaris, but instead about how to score a good deal on airline tickets and where the best Christmas decorations are in Omaha. I wrote about the National Mississippi River Museum in Dubuque so many times that I felt like I owned the place. I was accurate in the details and always met deadlines, which counted for more than writing talent in the sort of freelancing I was doing.

I found that Iowa was a surprisingly good place to be a travel writer. There weren't very many of us, for one thing, unlike in places such as San Francisco or New York. And while the famed Iowa Writers Workshop was full of people who wanted to publish short stories in the *New Yorker* or poems in literary magazines, they weren't interested in writing about dog-friendly hotels in Des Moines.

Once I had enough publications on my resume, I applied for membership in the Midwest Travel Journalists Association. That's when travel writing went from being fun to addictive—and why Indianapolis, which hosted the first MTJA conference I attended, will always have a rosy glow around it for Bob and me.

Bob had a bad back and so I drove the five-hour route with him lying nearly horizontal in the passenger seat. As we entered the outskirts of Indianapolis, a heavy rain began and I had to stop the car every few minutes to pull the windshield wiper back into place on the driver's side of our decrepit car. At one point we passed a vehicle in flames on the side of the road, the fire blazing despite the downpour.

Finally we arrived at the hotel, the best one in the city, and at the registration table for the conference received badges that were as magical as the golden tickets in *Willy Wonka & the Chocolate Factory*. As long as we wore them, we were the recipients of a fire hose of largesse. We had front row seats in a comedy club, enjoyed private tours of the city's best museums, ate in posh restaurants with unlimited glasses of wine, were guests of honor at a pioneer wedding at a living history farm, and rode in a race car at the Indianapolis Motor Speedway. For a couple who watched every penny of our spending and lived in a basement apartment, it was a somewhat surreal itinerary.

The trip was life-changing for both of us, a point when fate approached us with an engaging smile, uplifted eyebrow, and beckoning finger, inviting us to step into a world larger and richer than we'd known before. The intoxicating part wasn't the luxury, but the experiences.

We also loved the other travel writers, who were friendly and welcoming, curious about the world, good at asking questions, and full of interesting stories. Like me, most of them came from modest backgrounds. Some were the children of businessmen and insurance agents; others were retired from careers in public relations or education. Most of them said they lived simply when they weren't traveling.

"Travel writers are like wolves," one of them told me. "It's feast or famine. We eat when we can."

That first conference gave me connections that I used to get more work. I spent years writing primarily about Iowa and Midwestern destinations, mixing travel articles with assignments that paid better but weren't nearly as much fun. After our two sons, Owen and Carl, were born, I balanced my writing with carpooling, soccer games, and being a Cub Scout mom.

In those days of childrearing, it was always liberating to leave town. It didn't matter where I went—Columbus, Minneapolis, St. Louis, Milwaukee, wherever—because nearly every place was new to me. I loved exploring unfamiliar territory, especially in the company of the nomadic band of travel writer friends I'd made. These trips also gave me an excuse to be away from my children, whom I adored but who were relentless in the ways that small children are. Our friend Lisa took them occasionally for overnights so Bob and I could get away together, a gift that kept our marriage fresh and both of us sane.

As our boys grew older, I sought out family travel assignments that included them. We went on a re-creation of the Oregon Trail in western Nebraska, visited the Kennedy Space Center in Florida, and toured the Mark Twain sites in Hannibal, Missouri. Owen and Carl were dragged through endless museums, were coached by me to say memorable things that I then quoted in articles, and learned that they could order anything on the menu when Mom was on assignment but not when we were paying for it ourselves.

After 15 years of writing, and hundreds of articles about the Midwest, I was eager to travel more widely and broaden my professional connections. I applied for membership in the Society of American Travel Writers (SATW), a much larger organization than the Midwestern group, with members whose credentials made mine look embarrassingly amateurish. As I prepared to attend my first SATW convention in Dresden, Germany, I resolved to keep a low profile and learn as much as I could without drawing attention to myself.

Because my plane was late, I had just a few minutes in my hotel room to freshen up before going to the opening reception. Distracted and tired, I mixed up the cleaning and soaking solutions for my contacts—which I discovered when I popped the first lens in my eye. After yelping in pain and washing out my eye as best as I could, I was still determined to get to that reception, which I knew included representatives from the German government as well as hundreds of my new colleagues. I put my glasses back on, grabbed a handful of tissues, and sprinted through the hotel to the convention center.

As I approached, I heard the opening bars of *The Star-Spangled Banner* being played. I stopped on the stairway going down into the main hall, put my hand over my heart, and dabbed at my still-weepy eye.

As the song played on, the thought occurred to me that I should figure out where the American flag was so I could look in the right direction as I sang. I found it, all right: it was hanging from the railing right where I was standing. And on the floor below were 400 people looking up at me, no doubt wondering why I was so emotionally affected by the national anthem.

It was a memorable introduction, one that is still recalled with amusement by the friends I made in the organization once they realized I didn't have an Evita Perón complex after all.

Thanks to my expanding network of connections, gradually my work took me farther afield. I still wasn't making much money, but my travels became more exotic. I realized just how much my career had changed the day I flew into Orlando for a travel writers conference and got into the hotel shuttle. As I entered, I saw several other writers I knew.

"We missed you in Madrid!"

"Did you ever get that flight home from Cairo?"

"Are you going to New Zealand?"

As we chatted, the one non-travel-writer passenger in the van looked on us with growing puzzlement and finally asked who were. When we explained we were in the city for a travel writers conference, she sighed. "I'm here for a meeting of real estate agents," she said. "You guys are making me really depressed."

Packing the Sacred In Your Suitcase

I can pinpoint the exact moment my interest in writing about spiritual travel was born. I was browsing a magazine, one full of ads for cruises and articles on Five Perfect Days in Tahiti. But near the back I read an article of a different sort: it was about staying in retreat centers, primarily monasteries, across the U.S.

The article was a revelation. I hadn't even known that I could stay in a monastery, unless, you know, I was thinking of joining one. But it turns out that such places welcome visitors, and that the retreat business is booming for many of them. While the number of nuns and monks is going down, the number of people who want to experience the serenity of these communities is going up. The article reported that such places are often booked months in advance.

I looked up from my reading and said to myself, "That's what I want to write about."

So began my career as a travel writer specializing in holy sites. While I do other bread-and-butter writing projects that help pay the bills, much of my time is devoted to writing about the many places in the world where people can experience the holy—a fulfilling blend of my long-standing interest in spirituality and my passion for travel.

Essentially what I write about is pilgrimage, which is one of those pious words that scares some people off because they're afraid they're going to have to walk over rocks in bare feet and eat hardtack for six months. It's actually less esoteric than that. Most travelers have already been on a pilgrimage once or twice in their lives, whether they know it or not—when they visited the town where they grew up and walked its streets with a full heart, for example, seeing everything through the lens of memory. Or when they took a trip with a friend facing something big and scary, like a serious cancer diagnosis, and along with the fun was the knowledge of a powerful undertow just beneath the surface, making every stop for ice cream and view of a sunset bittersweet. Such trips are pilgrimages because they touch the heart and soul. There's nothing wrong with an ordinary vacation; sometimes what we need most is a beach, a mystery novel, and a gin and tonic. But at other times—which tend to come after losses and at transition points like graduations, decade birthdays, and retirements—the road calls to us in a different way. Even if we think we're not religious, even if we're skeptical of any kind of spirituality, something in our DNA draws us to wayfaring. I suspect it's part of what first drew our ancestors out of the trees on the savannas of Africa and eventually to every corner of the earth.

The sacred enters our lives through the tiniest of openings, often slipping in underneath a door that slams shut: the job ends, the lover leaves, the friendship dissolves into bitterness. Or the call may come through the comment of a stranger at a bus stop or in a headline we happen to read at a checkout counter. We tell ourselves we're foolish for listening to that inner urging, and yet we pack our bags and set out.

Pilgrimage is a nearly universal practice in religion, with Muslims journeying to Mecca and Jews to the Western Wall in Jerusalem while Christians walk in the footsteps of Jesus and the saints. Hindus travel to the Kumbh Mela, a festival said to be the world's largest religious gathering, while Buddhists go to Bodh Gaya in India where the Buddha attained enlightenment.

Whether a seeker sets out alone on a deserted trail or travels in the company of like-minded souls, pilgrimage is both an outer and inner journey. Ordinary trips bring a change in scenery; pilgrimages are meant to trigger a change of heart.

Especially in the pre-modern world, a pilgrim had to be a little crazy even to consider setting out from home. Because travelling was so treacherous, pilgrims would put their affairs in order before they left: they would pay outstanding debts, write their wills, and make provisions for dependents. In the Middle Ages, it was traditional that

Christian pilgrims would be blessed by a priest and anointed with holy water. If they died on the trip, they'd be ready to meet their maker, having squared both earthly and spiritual accounts.

The rigors and dangers of pilgrimage included robbers, rivers that had to be crossed on tipsy ferries, high mountain passes battered by winds and snow storms, ocean journeys plagued by seasickness and shipwrecks, and overnights in inns that were riddled with vermin, lice, and bedbugs. Anyone who's ever complained about hotel accommodations on a package tour should contemplate what it was like to travel for most of human history.

Such trips were sometimes undertaken as a form of penance (forgive me, Lord, for sleeping with my brother-in-law) or to fulfill a promise made to God after the fulfillment of a prayer (thanks so much for my recovery from smallpox). If pilgrims suffered some along the way, all the better, for the experience likely made them realize their dependence upon divine providence. We should never forget that *travel* and *travail* share the same root.

The popularity of pilgrimage has waxed and waned through the centuries, flourishing during the Middle Ages and declining during the Reformation and the Age of Enlightenment. But even at its lowest point, it never disappeared completely, and today we may be entering a new era of pilgrimage, despite (or perhaps because of) the growing disillusionment with organized religion. Especially in Christianity, people are finding on the road what they cannot find in churches.

And one of the truths of pilgrimage is this: often its most important part is not the destination, but what happens on the way.

❧

Let's go back to Concord once more—to Sleepy Hollow Cemetery, which is one of the world's great literary pilgrimage sites. The authors whose lives and careers were intertwined in the nineteenth century rest together here, neighbors in death as they were in life.

I found it interesting how the graves reflect the identities of each writer. Ralph Waldo Emerson's grave is designated by a massive boulder of uncut stone, a dramatic contrast to the neat rows of conventional grave markers that surround it. Its size recalls Emerson's status—no one's going to ignore this monument as they walk through the cemetery—but it also reflects his love of nature. Nathaniel Hawthorne's marker is much more modest, one that would likely meet approval from his stern Puritan ancestors. Louisa May Alcott's includes an American flag and a plaque identifying her as a veteran of the Civil War, a recognition of her time serving wounded soldiers as a nurse.

When I came to the corner of the cemetery where America's most famous prophet of simplicity rests, I was at first disappointed by the sight of a large, impressive monument bearing the name Thoreau, because it seemed out of keeping with his humble habits. Coming closer, I was relieved to find it bore the names of his relatives and that nearby was a much smaller marker with a single name: Henry. In death, as in life, Henry David Thoreau doesn't take up much real estate.

Here's what touched me the most. Scattered around the simple stone were pencils, pens, and scraps of paper on which people had written their favorite passages from his works. I've been at many other shrines around the world where people have left symbols of their devotion—prayers, crosses, photographs of loved ones, flowers—but never an array of writing utensils. Thoreau likely would complain about the waste of perfectly good pens and pencils, but I also imagine him being pleased that after all these years, his words still draw people here, to this serene spot beneath tall trees.

Sanctuary of Our Lady of Lourdes in France

CHAPTER 4

OF HEALING AND MIRACLES

Where there is great love there are always miracles.
Willa Cather

~ PILGRIMAGE ~
The Sanctuary of Our Lady of Lourdes in France

The ending of my tenure as a Wiccan coincided with a return to middle class respectability in my love life: after four years of living together, Bob and I got married. My parents, to my great relief, had gradually realized during those years that Bob was a gem—an unconventional one, to be sure, but a gem nonetheless. They often didn't understand a word he was saying, especially when he went off on an extended philosophical discourse, but there was genuine love between them.

"You can count on Bob," my father told me. "He's a hard worker and knows how to use tools. He's a good man to have around."

Back on the spiritual ranch, the next pony I rode was Buddhism. So much about it appealed to me: the writings of spiritual masters like the Dalai Lama and Thich Nhat Hanh, the centered calmness of many of its practitioners, the minimalist aesthetic, the graceful robes. In my social circle, it was also fashionable.

In the progressive enclave of Iowa City, where the Church of *The New York Times* is the preferred option on Sunday mornings, various forms of faith are ranked from ghastly to acceptable-as-long-as-you-aren't-too-enthusiastic. The list goes something like this:

10. Snake Handlers
9. Christian Fundamentalists Who Don't Believe in Evolution and Want to Take Over the U.S. Government
8. Jehovah's Witnesses
7. Baptists (the Southern ones, as most people don't realize they come in other flavors)
6. Catholics (their churches are a good place to go on Christmas to give the kids a cultural education)
5. Lutherans (they get a bump up because of the Garrison Keillor/NPR connection)
4. Methodists (good neighbors and they're unlikely ever to bring up religion in your presence)
3. Unitarian Universalists (they'll marry and bury anyone)
2. Secular Jews (engaging conversationalists)
1. Zen Buddhists (if a person is inexplicably interested in having a spiritual affiliation, this is as inoffensive as any)

Clearly the Buddhists were the coolest kids in the lunchroom. But an obstacle loomed large on my way to enlightenment: meditation, which I found to be the easiest thing in the world to do for about a minute and after that nearly impossible. I was hopeful for a while, thinking that the next new technique, book, or workshop would do the trick and I could sit on a cushion for more than five minutes. Nothing worked.

During this period, as I approached my 30s, I'd have latched onto indigenous spiritual traditions if even one of my ancestors hadn't been so intent on bonding with their fellow Norwegians and instead had married a Native American. For many years I'd greatly admired Lakota culture, in particular, thanks to our frequent travels to see Bob's family in South Dakota. But I knew how often non-native people have appropriated their spiritual traditions without permission or cultural sensitivity. I didn't want to be a wannabe.

Domesticity was intervening as well. Bob and I were planning to start a family of our own, and both of us wanted to be part of a religious community that wasn't quite as esoteric as what I'd been dabbling in. I also found myself growing tired of flying solo in my religious life. I knew from long experience how easy it is to let spiritual practices lapse. You miss a few days, and then the days stretch into weeks and then months. I hoped joining a group would help sustain my commitment.

So we became part of the Unitarian Universalist Society, where we were happily ensconced for several years. Formed from a merger of the Universalist Church of America (founded in 1793) and the American Unitarian Association (dating back to 1825), the U.U.s have deep roots in American history. Thomas Starr King, a Unitarian Universalist minister of the mid-nineteenth century, is credited with this explanation for the difference between the two groups: "Universalists believe that God is too good to damn people, and the Unitarians believe that people are too good to be damned by God." Illustrious U.U.s include President John Adams, Ralph Waldo Emerson, Walt Whitman, Susan B. Anthony, Beatrix Potter, and Henry David Thoreau, my friend from Walden Pond (while Thoreau wasn't much of a joiner, if he was anything, he was a Unitarian).

We grew to love our local Unitarian Universalist community, which met in an aging brick building with a minimally ornamented sanctuary that was vaguely churchy but not enough to give anyone the heebie-jeebies if they disliked Christianity. In this group my religious background wasn't unusual, since many of my fellow U.U.s had explored a variety of traditions. We'd trade stories of our experiences with different groups:

"Wicca? Great—love that Starhawk stuff."

"I'm actually Bahá'í, but the U.U.s are as close as I can get in Iowa City."

"I was raised Catholic and then became an Evangelical, and now I don't believe in anything, but I love coming here on Sunday mornings."

After our son, Owen, was born—in a Catholic hospital, where I first double-checked to confirm that I'd gotten the whole save-the-baby-let-the-mother-die thing wrong—we had a joyous naming ceremony for him, the U.U. equivalent of baptism. Many of the rituals there felt like Christianity-through-the-looking-glass, similar on the surface but different in fundamental ways. During a period of silence in the middle of the service people were invited to reflect or pray, for example, but most Sundays I was just getting quiet and settled when it was time to move on. And the hymnal at first perusal looked like that of the Lutheran Church, only instead of songs about sin and redemption it had tunes scrubbed so clean of Christian and sexist language that I suspected there was a full-time bureaucrat in the U.U. headquarters whose job was to redact lyrics like the C.I.A. censors intelligence reports.

We appreciated the eclectic vibe of the services, which were often created and led by members of the congregation. We liked the sermons, too, which focused on practical and political topics, from how to raise children in a media-saturated culture to discussions of welfare reform.

The U.U.s taught me that a big part of being in a religious community is simply showing up. Even on the Sundays when I'd rather sleep in, or on weekday nights when I was unenthusiastic about going to a committee meeting, I always gained something from making the effort. Bob and I served on committees, taught children's religious education classes, and pitched in on volunteer projects.

What I liked best was coffee hour after the services. People would exclaim over how sweet our baby was and I enjoyed connecting with the other mothers, who tended to be equally passionate about breast-feeding, organic foods, yoga, and the very real possibility that their child was a prodigy. Each week I'd learn who was pregnant and who had received a cancer diagnosis, who needed a ride to a doctor's appointment on Wednesday, and who had just read a book she was certain I'd like. We looked forward to many years of being part of that warm and lively community.

And then Owen got sick.

❧

Our first son had been born healthy and strong. But at the age of five months, what seemed like a case of the flu rapidly degenerated into bacterial meningitis. Within 24 hours of the first symptoms, Owen was having seizures. After an emergency room visit to our neighborhood hospital, where a spinal tap showed that a deadly infection was attacking his brain, he was taken by ambulance to the pediatric intensive care unit at the University of Iowa Hospital. There he was put on intravenous antibiotics while his medical team closely monitored his condition. He remained unresponsive and still, surrounded by machines and hooked up to a network of tubes and wires.

It was a nightmare.

After four days in the hospital, a colleague of Bob's came to visit. I didn't know her well, but when she asked if she could pray at Owen's bedside, it gave me some comfort. She remained at his side for about 15 minutes, standing quietly with her eyes closed.

As she exited the room, she smiled at us. "This room is full of prayers," she said. "I can feel that Owen is surrounded by divine protection."

I was struck by her calm. It wasn't her baby near death, but still, she had a tranquility that made me hopeful that perhaps Owen would emerge from this crisis healthy and whole.

I prayed too. Endlessly. The rest of the world ceased to exist and all that mattered was right in front of us: Owen, pale and motionless. The IV line with its steady drip of fluids. The beeping of monitors. The frequent checks by nurses. Hour after hour after hour after hour. While there may be no atheists in foxholes, there aren't very many in pediatric intensive care units either.

It was astonishing how dramatically our world had changed in such a short time. Friends brought us food. I hadn't showered in days. I kept losing track of what day of the week it was. We met a few of the other parents in the ICU, people as shell-shocked as we were. We connected with one family in particular, parents of a little boy with a head injury, sustained in a farm accident. We traded reports of how our sons were doing, measuring their incremental improvements on the smallest of scales.

After a week it became clear that Owen would live. His physicians, however, tried to prepare us for the fact we may not get the old Owen back. Brain scans and other tests showed some problems, including deafness in one ear, a common side effect of the type of meningitis he had. There may be other damage as well, they said, carefully choosing their words. They would need to track him as he grew to make sure there were no developmental delays.

As Owen came out of his coma, he did indeed appear changed. Before becoming ill he'd been a normal, happy baby, but now he was listless and unresponsive. We sat by the side of his bed and continually searched his face for clues of what the future held. I had cried so much I felt like a dried-out husk.

A Raccoon Brings Resurrection

Before Owen's illness, a raccoon puppet had been one of his favorite toys, and once he emerged from the coma we brought it to the hospital. I was playing with it one afternoon as I stood by Owen's bedside, making the arms move, shaking its head from side to side, trying to get Owen to respond. Finally he did, a little—a fleeting smile crossed his face. And then a bigger smile.

Over the next hour, Bob and I watched in awe and amazement as Owen went through all of the developmental milestones of his first five months. It was like seeing a time lapse video of a blossoming flower. He had an IV line in a vein on his forehead, protected by half of a Styrofoam cup taped over it, making him look like a little Shriner wearing a cock-eyed cap. His appearance added to our delight in what was happening. He babbled, he began to laugh, he reached out his hands to us. He came back to life.

We had our baby back. We didn't fully relax—that would come later when it became apparent that Owen had come through his ordeal intact except for the deafness in one ear—but the relief and joy of that hour remains one of the happiest memories of my life.

The next day our U.U. minister visited us in Owen's hospital room. Like all the people in our church community, he'd been greatly worried and was relieved to see that Owen was getting better. He was a kind, caring, and loving man. But as we sat in the hospital room together, all he could say was several variations of, "I'm so sorry this has happened."

As he left the room, I felt deflated. That was it? No prayers, no putting this in a larger context, no words of comfort? Just that he was sorry this had happened? It wasn't much to get from a religious community to which I'd devoted years of my life.

I realize now my reaction was mediated by lack of sleep and being wrung out by worry. I know many U.U. congregations have a strong spiritual sense, ones that would have had a different response to Owen's illness. But ours at the time was more secular humanist than spiritual, and when we needed help the most, it wasn't there for us. We craved more than the warm bonds of community: we needed help in creating meaning from that crisis. We didn't want platitudes or a facile theology, but rather an acknowledgement that we'd encountered a deep mystery and that our lives wouldn't be the same again.

Something changed within me during the two weeks we spent with Owen in the hospital, a shift that marked the beginning of the end of our time as Unitarian Universalists.

A Sacred Spring at the Town Dump

Although more than a decade had passed since Owen's illness, memories of that dark time kept returning to me during a trip to Lourdes, Christianity's most famous healing shrine. In Lourdes, I recalled the days when I was the one praying desperately for a miracle.

I was in France on a writing assignment, accompanied by my friend Catherine, who shares my passion for visiting holy places. After touring sites in the northern part of the country, we'd headed south by car, eventually coming to Lourdes in the foothills of the Pyrenees Mountains. As we entered its outskirts, we could see dozens of hotels, the plethora of lodging places reminding me of the universal truth that while pilgrimage sites are good for the soul, they're also good for business.

After checking into our own hotel, we set off on foot towards the shrine. With every block the streets grew more crowded, and as people passed by I heard snatches of conversation in many languages. Soon I saw shops stocked with every kind of religious souvenir: rosaries, calendars, candles, paperweights, jewelry, and crosses. Others sold containers to hold water from Lourdes' famous spring and Virgin Mary statues arranged by size on the shelves, as if she had a dozen identical sisters born a year apart.

I recalled the comment of a friend who'd visited Lourdes: "You're going to love the shrine and hate the shops," she said. "Be prepared for endless kitsch."

Instead, to my surprise I loved the stores, as I found all the images of Mary strangely appealing. Everywhere I looked—on postcards by the cash registers, emblazoned on pens and coffee cups, smiling beatifically on posters—she gazed at me, serene and welcoming. "How wonderful you're finally here," she seemed to be saying.

I was moved, too, by watching those who were purchasing the trinkets and statues, the elderly women carefully counting out their change and the earnest young people buying handfuls of cheap holy medals. I imagined the places these tokens would end up, how they'd find their way into nursing homes, hospital rooms, and bedside drawers, into the pockets of chemotherapy patients and the hands of the dying. It didn't make any difference that they were mass-produced in places far away from Lourdes. Everyone could take Mary home, because she was as present in a pocket-sized plastic statue as a cathedral.

As we continued walking, the commercial district ended and we reached the entrance to the shrine. Just inside St. Joseph's Gate, a large marble statue depicted Mary appearing to a patient in a hospital bed, a man who didn't look nearly as startled as I would be under those circumstances. A few more steps and a basilica came into view, an imposing structure with a huge, gilded crown set atop its lower level. Two ramps extended like arms from each side, ending in a huge square and esplanade capable of holding many thousands of people. The scene blended piety and splendor with a dash of Disneyland.

People were everywhere. Some wore long robes, nuns' habits, or clerical collars that marked them as the professionally religious. Most were European, while others hailed from countries much farther away. Gray-haired couples walked arm in arm, Italian women strolled by in furs and elegant shoes, and groups marched by with banners emblazoned with the names of their churches.

Most of all, I was struck by the many who were obviously at Lourdes in search of healing: people in wheelchairs pushed by family members; women with bald heads covered by scarves; disabled children; old men with limping gaits and faces lined by pain. It became clear to me that while Lourdes attracts pilgrims of many nationalities and social classes, this holy site belongs to the sick.

❦

Appropriately, I arrived at the shrine on February 11, the anniversary of the first apparition of the Virgin Mary at Lourdes in 1858. The story of that day illustrates the fact that when the holy comes to call, she often walks right past the church door to wander instead down a back alley in a rough part of town.

Bernadette Soubirous, who would soon astonish the world with her story of seeing the Virgin Mary not just once but 18 times, was a young woman with no social standing and few prospects. Sickly and asthmatic and the eldest of nine children, she worked as a hired servant and couldn't read or write. Her family lived in a room that had once been the town jail.

The 14-year-old Bernadette was gathering firewood at the base of a hill called Massabielle, the "old rock." This was hardly a peaceful place for contemplation: Bernadette's glorious visions happened in a spot where garbage was thrown and pigs rooted. Though accompanied by her sister and a friend, only Bernadette saw the vision. There came a sound like a rushing wind, and when she looked up she saw a figure in an indentation in the rock above her: a beautiful young woman, glowing with light.

"I saw a lady dressed in white," Bernadette would later recount. "She wore a white dress, with an equally white veil, a blue belt and a yellow rose on each foot."

Over the course of the next five months, Bernadette saw the figure again and again at Massabielle. Those who accompanied her never shared in the visions, but they could see that she was transfixed by them. Over time, the woman gradually revealed more about herself to Bernadette. She said she wanted people to pray and do penance and that a church should be built for her at the site. During one of her appearances, she told Bernadette to dig in the soil, and when the girl did, a spring appeared. During the sixteenth apparition she told Bernadette her name: "I am the Immaculate Conception." (Extra credit if you know that the Immaculate Conception doesn't refer to the virgin birth of Jesus, but rather to the theological doctrine that Mary was conceived without original sin.)

I know—this is a lot to swallow, especially if, like me, you started out with an ancestral distrust of Catholicism, followed by a chaser of Unitarian Universalism. But I loved the story of Bernadette's visions. There she was, little Bernadette, a Nobody from Nowhere, and yet she was the one chosen to receive the amazing visions. The Virgin Mary knew from personal experience that if you need something important done, young girls from rural areas are a surprisingly good choice.

Did Bernadette concoct the whole thing? If she did, I wonder why, since her life was pretty miserable after word got around about her visions. She may well have regretted telling people what she'd seen. At first she was scolded and persecuted for telling lies, and then she was hounded by people who believed her story and wanted to hear it again and again. Despite the endless repetitions, she never changed any significant details. When pressed for more information, she'd say, "I am here to tell you what happened. I am not here to make you believe."

One of the things I've learned in my travels is that religious visions typically bring a pack o' trouble with them. You may end up as a saint after you die—Bernadette was canonized in 1933, five decades after her death—but your life usually isn't made any easier by a divine revelation. Certainly the Virgin Mary was correct when she told Bernadette, "I do not promise to make you happy in this world but in the other."

Word quickly spread about the strange events in Lourdes, especially after a woman with an injured arm was healed after bathing it in the miraculous spring. Even those who didn't believe in the apparitions were willing to give the healing water a try, in part because of the primitive state of medical care in that era.

After at first distancing themselves from the events, church officials undertook a four-year investigation that led them to conclude that Bernadette's visions were authentic. In 1871 a church was built at the site to accommodate the steadily growing number of pilgrims. The spring uncovered by Bernadette was piped into baths in which the sick could be immersed and fountains where people could fill containers to take the healing water home with them. Sleepy little Lourdes was very different from what it had been when Bernadette received her first vision.

As for Bernadette, at the age of 22 she entered a convent in the town of Nevers, nearly 500 miles away from her hometown. She worked in its infirmary, caring for the sick despite her own poor health. Even though she'd founded the most important healing shrine in Christianity, she herself died young, succumbing to tuberculosis at the age of 35. The healing waters of Lourdes were for other pilgrims, but not for her.

I can't rationally explain the visions experienced by that poor, uneducated girl near the town dump. Yet I believe that something extraordinary happened in 1858, a shift in ordinary reality that still draws millions to Lourdes.

And it was somehow connected to the woman who'd smiled at me from the shelves of the gift stores outside the shrine, a figure who was becoming more real to me all the time.

Ordinary, Extraordinary Miracles

I remember a young woman I saw in the midst of the crowds near the holy spring. She knelt on the pavement, her eyes closed, oblivious to the light rain that was falling and the commotion around her. On her face was an expression of raw pleading that was so exposed, so intimate, that I felt I shouldn't witness it. I recognized that look, for I knew it had been mine when Owen was near death.

It's not surprising that many of the world's pilgrimage sites are associated with healing. While Lourdes is the best-known in the Christian faith, most shrines have a place where symbolic tokens are left by those seeking recovery from illness. When we—or loved ones—are seriously ill, the need for divine connection is so powerful that it can overcome even the most committed atheism. Make me well. Give us one more year with him. Let her live. The prayers come, even if we doubt there's anyone out there to receive them.

Before I left on my trip to Lourdes, a number of people asked me to pray for them there. Even my secular friends were intrigued, having heard that Lourdes is a place of miraculous healing. "I don't believe in miracles," they told me, but then they went on to ask me to pray for them or their loved ones there, just in case.

I was surprised to learn that the shrine tries to take a scientific approach to the miracles that happen there. A medical office staffed by an international team of health professionals closely examines each claim, documenting the illnesses and the treatments people have received, and then investigating whether the cure was complete and permanent. Only then will they pronounce the healing "inexplicable." It is up to the Roman Catholic Church to make the final determination of whether a miracle has occurred. To date, 69 miracles have been officially documented in this way at Lourdes.

The Church also recognizes that there's a difference between a physical cure and a healing of the spirit, which can happen independently of each other. An ill person may come to Lourdes and receive a profound gift of peacefulness and acceptance and then return home to die. These are the ordinary miracles that happen each day at Lourdes—though of course they're not ordinary at all to the people who receive them.

All I know is that when I stood before the rock where Bernadette received her visions, Lourdes didn't feel like a place of suffering, but of joy. Surrounded by pilgrims, many burdened by physical illness, others bearing sorrows of the heart, I felt as if we were all part of a grand parade of the broken, a community bound together by a love that emanated from the shrine.

That sense grew even stronger on my last morning at Lourdes, as I walked through the shrine saying goodbye to a place that had come to feel strangely like home over the course of a three-day visit. It was raining, but that didn't diminish the crowds of people at the grotto. I watched as a group of pilgrims gathered around a priest who was celebrating mass. A line of people formed to receive communion, and to my surprise the group began singing a hymn I knew very well: "A Mighty Fortress Is Our God."

I blinked back tears. Of all the places to hear that old Lutheran standard, I thought. As I stood looking at the worshippers, one of them beckoned me forward. "You, too," he said in accented English, inviting me to join the line.

Not being Catholic, I hadn't intended to receive communion at Lourdes. But the combination of the familiar hymn and the personal invitation drew me in. Sheltered from the rain by my umbrella, watched over by the Virgin Mary statue that stood in the grotto above me, and surrounded by Catholics singing a song written by the most famous Lutheran of them all, I received the consecrated bread.

On a pilgrimage, sometimes worlds intersect in most interesting and unexpected ways.

❧

Several years ago, Bob and I received an invitation to attend a farewell party for our family doctor, Ralph. After several decades in Iowa City, he was moving to another state and wanted to say goodbye to his patients. At the event we hugged him and told him how much his care had meant to us, especially during Owen's illness twenty years before. Ralph nodded. "You know, I never told you how bad the brain scans looked," he said. "I thought Owen was going to end up profoundly disabled. I couldn't bear to tell you." And then he added this: "I've been in practice for a long time, and there have been just a handful of times when something happened that I couldn't explain medically. Owen's recovery is one of them."

I've thought about Ralph's comment many times. Our baby came back to life again before our eyes. In thinking of this as a miracle, I know I'm entering murky theological waters. Why does one person receive a miracle, and another doesn't? I think of all the other patients in that pediatric intensive care ward, and of all the children who continue to suffer across the world today. I remember the little boy with the head injury in the hospital when Owen was ill, and I wonder if his parents are still praying for his recovery.

And yet to dismiss what happened to Owen as a medical fluke doesn't feel right either. George Bernard Shaw defined a miracle as an event that creates faith, but I think perhaps a better definition is that a miracle is an experience that evokes gratitude.

My son, who came close to dying, who so easily could have been left handicapped, is now a biomedical engineer. I sometimes think of what could have been, and I know this: if I could be granted just one miracle over the course of my life, this is the one I would choose. And for this miracle, I am profoundly, deeply, and everlastingly thankful.

Jerusalem

CHAPTER 5

IN THE LIGHT OF
STAINED GLASS WINDOWS

Go where your best prayers take you.
Frederick Buechner

~ PILGRIMAGE ~
Jerusalem and Galilee in Israel

The process of leaving the Unitarian Universalists took a couple of years and involved a fair amount of heartache. Many people have written about the pain of leaving fundamentalist churches, but in my experience, leaving a liberal one can be a wrenching process, too.

The prospect of leaving made me feel like a quitter, someone who couldn't be depended upon. And I knew that while I could see our fellow Unitarians in other social contexts, the easy camaraderie of these friendships depended upon regularly interacting with each other on Sunday mornings. Religious communities are formed in part upon a shared sense of who's on the inside and who's on the outside, and once someone leaves, relationships change.

At the same time, I had an ever-growing sense of restlessness, especially on Sunday mornings as I sat in the pew. For me this feeling is usually a sign of the spirit at work, but when I'm in the middle of the transformation it's no fun at all. I think I'm settled and then comes a nudge, a burr in the saddle, a stone in my shoe. I can't get comfortable. Things bother me that didn't before. I daydreamed about other churches when I should have been paying attention to the sermon. I was undergoing the religious equivalent of searching online dating sites while my spouse was asleep.

I'd finally found a spiritual community that fit me in many ways, especially the Unitarian openness to inspiration from many traditions. At the same time, I was beginning to feel that in all my wanderings through various faiths, I was like someone who'd picked up 100 words in five different languages. I could order from the menu in a fast food restaurant, but I couldn't understand complexities. And I reluctantly recognized that my first religious language was Christianity. Perhaps it was time to give Jesus another try.

If you're thinking this doesn't sound particularly enthusiastic, you're right. Christianity didn't have the most sterling of reputations, especially in the social circles in which I moved and during an era when the financial and sexual shenanigans of religious leaders like Jim and Tammy Faye Bakker and Jimmy Swaggart were making headlines. I didn't want to be associated with their cartoonish version of Christianity, but what made me even more hesitant was something else: Christianity was just so *dull*. Boring music, droning sermons, fussiness about small details, no sense of humor.

Nevertheless, I convinced Bob that we should give Christianity, the religion of both of our childhoods, another try. Before he agreed, though, he offered up one final alternative.

"Maybe we could try the Zen Center?" he asked hopefully.

I gestured toward Owen, who was making loud explosion sounds as he rammed two trucks together, and our newly born son Carl, wailing to be picked up.

"I'll tell you what," I replied. "First you teach the boys to meditate and then we'll join the Zen Center."

We visited a few churches, though none of them appealed to us very much. Then I remembered a conversation I'd had with our neighbor, Julia, several years before, during which she mentioned that she'd just finished reading the Bible again—the entire book, not just a few verses.

I was a little embarrassed for her. She was clearly an educated, liberal sort of person—an attorney, for goodness sake—and yet she was reading the Bible. But when we were church-shopping, I thought about that conversation and mentioned to her that I'd like to attend services with her sometime. She said it was the beginning of Lent and that I could go with her to the Ash Wednesday service that week at the downtown Episcopal church she and her family attended.

Lent? The term was vaguely familiar from my Lutheran days, but I wasn't sure what it referred to. But I was game to give it a try. While Bob stayed with the boys, I went to church with Julia.

Thus I showed up at All Saints Church (as I'll call it) on Ash Wednesday, the day that marks the beginning of the 40-day period leading up to Easter. It's the service where a priest puts a smudge of ash on your forehead and gives you the not-so-cheerful message, "From dust you came, and to dust you shall return." At All Saints that evening, there were also psalms and long prayers and multiple references to sin, and music that could not by any stretch of the imagination be described as catchy or upbeat. It felt foreign, but at the same time oddly appealing.

When I got home, Bob asked me how it had gone. "I'm not sure," I told him. "But whatever it was, it certainly wasn't Christianity Lite."

I couldn't quite explain it, but something about that service drew me back. The next Sunday we both attended, sitting in the back pew. After the service, the rector (an Episcopal term for pastor) came over to introduce himself. He'd changed out of the heavy, embroidered robe he'd worn during the service into a somber black shirt with a little white collar. The official church uniform made me wary—I very much hoped he wasn't going to quiz me on whether I'd asked Jesus to enter my heart—but he was down-to-earth and warm. When we said we didn't know much about the Episcopal Church, he reached into the holder on the back of the pew and held up a copy of the *Book of Common Prayer*.

"This is the heart of the Episcopal Church," he said. "It's got pretty much everything in it. If you look in the back, there's even a service for goat sacrifices."

Given Bob's history as the Most Famous Goat Farmer in America, and my own coat-of-many-colors religious identity, it was about the most inviting thing he could have said to us.

Sitting On a Three-Legged Stool

I jumped enthusiastically into the Episcopal pond, which is surprising given how different it was from my tenure with the Unitarian Universalists. Perhaps I was simply ready for a change, but I soon fell in love with the solemnity and grandeur of the Episcopal Church.

While the Unitarian Universalist ambiance was relaxed, the Episcopal style was much more formal. The Eucharist was held each Sunday, a service in which bread and wine are consecrated as the body and blood of Christ. The liturgy began with a solemn procession of white-robed acolytes, choir members, and clergy, all walking behind a gold cross held high above people's heads on a staff.

Organ music, pews with kneelers, stained glass windows, and an altar set with gleaming silver pieces were additional reminders that I'd wandered far from the Unitarian fold. The sanctuary had soaring wooden beams and a stained glass window of Jesus as the Good Shepherd above its altar, with brass memorial plaques on its walls giving credit to long-dead, generous Episcopalians.

Over the next months we gradually learned to find our way through the *Book of Common Prayer*, whose language can be traced back to a 1549 collection of prayers compiled during the reign of the English King Edward VI. As a writer, I appreciated the beauty of its prose, which was dignified and stately, a counterpoint to the architecture of All Saints.

One of the first Episcopal terms I encountered was *via media*, Latin for "the middle way," a philosophy that in many ways defines the denomination. The Episcopal Church is a hybrid of Catholic and Protestant traditions, having been born in the sixteenth century when the Church of England split from Rome. The Pope had refused to grant King Henry VIII an annulment of his marriage when he wished to marry again to produce a male heir. The English monarch made himself head of the church, but much remained of Catholic practices. Anglicanism (as the Episcopal Church is known in most of the larger world) has sought ever since to be a golden mean between the two main branches of Western Christianity. It has considerable uniformity in its worship but a great deal of latitude for individual conscience. The classic description of the Anglican way is that it is a three-legged stool, relying equally on scripture, tradition, and reason.

All Saints was intellectual but not stuffy, an atmosphere set by the rector who'd greeted us on our first Sunday. Jason had an opera-quality baritone voice, keen sense of liturgical theater, love of people, and wicked sense of humor (the *Book of Common Prayer* does not, in fact, contain a service for goat sacrifices).

As one of the downtown's historic churches, All Saints attracted a mix of university professors, librarians, and medical professionals, people who were both well-educated and serious about their faith. That was most evident during the Sunday morning adult education hour, which explored challenging topics spanning a broad range of social, political, and theological themes. I soon learned that it was O.K. to ask hard questions as an Episcopalian. In fact, at All Saints it was a badge of honor. The one hazard was that no matter what topic was discussed, there was a good chance someone in the group had done a PhD on that subject—or one at least tangentially related—and could launch into an extended lecture given even the most minimal of encouragement.

The more I got to know the members of All Saints, the more their quirkiness became evident. There was Rusty, who each year hosted a large outdoor tea party to celebrate the Queen of England's birthday, with women in extravagant hats and men in ties and suit coats nibbling on lemon curd tarts and Scottish shortbread. The choir director, a man of fearsomely high musical standards, wasn't very interested in us once we confessed we couldn't sing well, but he adored compliments, gazing rapturously at us in a way that egged us on to ever greater superlatives. And I appreciated it when a couple of elderly women instructed me in the nuances of how to host Episcopal coffee hours, which served a brand of coffee called Bishop's Blend and a wider range of snacks than the Unitarian Universalists did.

"The Good Lord wants us to *enjoy* ourselves," one of them told me. "And I think he appreciates having food served on nice plates and napkins, too."

Having been raised as a practical Lutheran, I was struck by the lack of commonsense know-how in the congregation, among whom knowledge of basic carpentry skills was far less common than a familiarity with the theological controversies settled by the seventh-century Synod of Whitby. But it meant that Bob's handyman skills were welcomed with great appreciation, as he was the rare parishioner who could straddle the philosophical and practical realms.

The months passed, and Bob and I settled into our new identities as Christians. On Sunday mornings, we flipped back and forth to the right parts of the prayer book with ease, joined in on the hymns, received communion, and knelt at the appropriate points in the service. I was amused to realize that an observer could easily have mistaken us for cradle Episcopalians.

Tending the Theological Chickens

On a visit to our boys' Sunday School room one morning, I overheard Owen giving a lesson to Carl on the geography of the Holy Land, using a map of the region with small tokens designating various sites.

First Owen picked up a cross, showed it to his brother, and placed it in the middle of Jerusalem, saying, "Carl, this is a cross, and it goes *here*." Then he picked up a star-shaped token, again showed it to his wide-eyed brother, and placed it in Bethlehem as he said with great authority, "Carl, this is a chicken, and it goes *here*."

During those first years at All Saints, I found that much of my knowledge of Christianity was the equivalent of Owen confusing the Star of Bethlehem with a chicken. I'd studied other faiths with enthusiasm and no small amount of rigor, but not the religion of my childhood. A lot of what I thought I knew about Christianity was a hodgepodge of half-remembered doctrines and impressions absorbed from popular culture.

Religions have many entry points, I've since come to realize. For some people the call to belong comes through a dynamic preacher, soul-stirring music, a profound epiphany, or simply the comfort of having been in a pew nearly every Sunday since they were born. For me, it was the storytelling skills of Jesus that most captured my attention.

Hearing the Gospel stories with fresh ears was an advantage. I'd often sit in church amazed by how an uneducated carpenter from Podunk, Galilee, was able to spin metaphors, convey deep insights into human psychology, sketch universal dramas with economy and wit, and teach profound truths through parables. Jesus took the ordinary and held it up to the light so that people could see the sacred shining through.

The parable that affected me most deeply, the one that kept coming back to me at unexpected times, was that of the Prodigal Son, found in the Gospel of Luke. The phrase has passed into common usage to the point that most of us think we know the full story when we don't, because it's like one of those sets of Russian dolls nested within each other, with new truths revealed at each level.

The story is about a wealthy man with two sons. The younger asks to have his inheritance early, which even today would be a mark of arrogance and in the patriarchal society of Jesus' day was an especially grave offense. But the father agrees, and the son travels to a far country and lives a wild life, wasting his entire fortune. He's so poor that he's reduced to sharing food with the pigs. Destitute and despairing, he decides that he'll go back to his father and ask to be taken on as a hired hand, knowing that he's no longer worthy to be called his father's son.

As he approaches his home, his father sees him in the distance and runs toward him with open arms. "Bring him the best robe and kill the fatted calf so that we may have a feast to celebrate!" he cries. "For this son of mine was dead and is alive again!"

Most secular people think the story ends here, in this feel-good, Hallmark movie sort of climax. But Jesus continues the story by describing the elder son's reaction. He's been watching all of this drama with resentment and envy. "I have done what you asked and have never caused you any trouble," he says to the father, "and yet you have never had a feast for me. And here is my brother who has squandered your money and yet you welcome him like this."

And the father, who loves them both, says, "My son, you are always with me, and everything I have is yours. But we had to celebrate and be glad, because your brother was dead and is alive again; he was lost and is found."

The parable illustrates two meanings of the word *prodigal*. The son is prodigal in the most common sense of the word, meaning that he's wasteful and reckless. But the father is prodigal in one of its lesser-known meanings: he gives his love on a lavish scale, exhibiting an overflowing, unstinting generosity of spirit. Through this story, Jesus reminds his listeners that God is always willing to welcome us back, no matter what we have done, no matter how far we have strayed—and that God always gives us more love than we can possibly deserve.

You're probably thinking that I most identified with the younger son, being the lapsed Lutheran-Wiccan-Unitarian that I was. But that wasn't the case, as I never considered myself lost during my years of religious journeying. No, the person I most identified with in the story was the elder son: the dutiful child, the one who thought he was doing everything right, the guy who was probably voted Boy Citizen of his Nazareth High School Class of 20 AD.

To me the most compelling aspect of the parable was how Jesus managed to capture two ways of being spiritually lost. There's the obvious one—the bad choices and selfish indulgences that lead to ruin—and the more subtle, pernicious version, in which we're bulwarked with pride and arrogance and steeped in resentment. Of the two, the latter is almost always the more difficult to overcome. Tellingly, Jesus doesn't reveal what happens to the elder brother. Was he able to listen to his father's message and embrace his brother in love? Jesus certainly implies that the older son's repentance is no sure thing.

One mark of a profound story is how it speaks to people through generations and across cultures. Take, for example, what happened to Henri Nouwen, a Dutch Catholic priest, theologian, and author, when he became fascinated with this parable.

In his book *The Return of the Prodigal Son: A Story of Homecoming,* Nouwen writes of coming home exhausted after a six-week lecture tour in 1983. On the door of a friend's office he happened to see a poster of a Rembrandt painting depicting a scene from the parable: the elderly father has his hands upon the shoulders of the son who kneels before him, gently welcoming him back from his exile. To the side are several figures in the shadows, looking with enigmatic expressions at the reunion.

Nouwen was transfixed by this painting, particularly by the expression of infinite compassion and forgiveness on the face of the father and by the brokenness of the son who leans into his embrace. The painting triggered in him an immense longing for comfort, belonging, and peace.

The moment passed, but Nouwen's fascination with the painting and the parable remained. His ruminations on both helped crystalize for him a decision to change the direction of his life, to leave behind his academic career to join a L'Arche community in Canada, one of an international network of homes and programs helping those with intellectual disabilities.

The lure of the painting was so powerful that Nouwen eventually traveled to Saint Petersburg (then known as Leningrad) to see the original in the Hermitage Museum. He was granted special permission to remain with Rembrandt's masterwork for much longer than an ordinary tourist would. Over the course of two days he spent more than four hours sitting in front of the eight-by-six-feet canvas, watching as the light played across its surface, illuminating new details as it shifted across the painting.

As Nouwen sat there, hour after hour, he pondered aspects of himself that were revealed in each of the paintings' characters. He reflected on how at times he'd been the younger son squandering blessings and needing forgiveness, and at other times the elder brother filled with disdain and envy. And he came to realize that the painting is an invitation to take on another identity as well: that of the Father overflowing with divine compassion and love.

Of all the details in Rembrandt's painting, Nouwen kept coming back to the father's hands, bathed in luminous light:

> From the moment I first saw the poster . . . I felt drawn to those hands. I did not fully understand why. But gradually over the years I have come to know those hands. They have held me from the hour of my conception, they welcomed me at my birth, held me close to my mother's breast, fed me, and kept me warm. They have protected me in times of danger and consoled me in times of grief. They have waved me good-bye and always welcomed me back. Those hands are God's hands. They are also the hands of my parents, teachers, friends, healers, and all those whom God has given me to remind me how safely I am held.

In church, I often felt like Nouwen sitting in front of Rembrandt's painting, watching and marveling at what I was seeing in Christianity for the first time. I had missed so much before. I was making up for lost time.

The Holy Land at Breakneck Speed

During this time of re-learning what I thought I knew about Christianity, I traveled to Israel. Because I was with a group of travel writers, my trip was hardly ideal for spiritual reflection, but I still hoped to squeeze in a few prayers along the way.

With more sacred sites per square inch than anywhere else on earth, the Holy Land attracts pilgrims from three of the world's great religions, who come to see sites ranging from the Jewish Western Wall and the Muslim Dome of the Rock to Christianity's Church of the Holy Sepulchre. Our first day in Jerusalem illustrated a common problem of many guided tours, which too often put centuries of history into a blender and spit them out at high speed. We saw the Mount of Olives-Garden of Gethsemane-Western Wall-Church of All Nations-Church of the Holy Sepulchre-Garden Tomb in one day. I knew quite a bit about Jewish and Christian history before arriving, but even I was confused by the barrage of information. I kept mixing up the Sadducees with the Samaritans and I had to struggle to keep track of who-was-who among the many badly behaving relatives of Herod the Great.

"This has been one of those days when I'm glad I write about golf courses," a fellow travel writer told me that evening while we were visiting about our respective specialties.

I was relieved to have the next day free to explore the city at my own pace. A short walk from our hotel brought me to the walled Old City, where I stepped into a labyrinth of streets, alleyways, and cave-like merchants stalls, the air filled with the smells of spices, cooking meats, and the musty decay of old buildings. As I walked I passed a steady stream of people: Jews wearing tefillin, black-robed Greek Orthodox nuns, Israeli soldiers with guns slung behind their backs, groups of Christian pilgrims in matching T-shirts, and elderly Muslims fingering prayer beads. With so much history and conflicting political agendas coming together in the Old City, its humming vitality contained a hint of unease, and I recalled the description of the city given by the first-century Roman-Jewish historian Josephus: Jerusalem, he said, is a golden bowl full of scorpions.

As I walked, I traced the Via Dolorosa, the Way of Sorrow, which marks the path followed by Jesus from the Roman judgment court, known as the Praetorium, to Golgotha. The route includes fourteen stations, nine along the narrow streets and five inside the Church of the Holy Sepulchre, the place where Jesus is believed to have died and been resurrected.

Was this the exact route taken by Jesus? Probably not, our guide had told us. But as with so much in Israel, historical exactitude is not the point. Jesus did walk through the city on his way to be killed, and then, as now, Jerusalem was a bustling place, full of the cajoling of shopkeepers and the busyness of people going about their ordinary routines. The normal rhythms of Jerusalem did not stop for that tortured journey, and neither does the Old City keep quiet for the pilgrims who reverently walk the Via Dolorosa today.

My experiences in the Old City mirror that of many pilgrims visiting popular holy sites: how does one manage to be devout and prayerful in a crowded, noisy place? It's hard enough to get into that groove in a quiet church, but just try finding it sandwiched between a vendor yelling about how delicious his freshly squeezed orange juice is and another hawking bargains on olive wood crucifixes and menorahs.

The question loomed even larger once I came to the Church of the Holy Sepulchre, one of the most important pilgrimage sites in Christianity. Inside its huge wooden doors were crowds of people, some in a reverential mood and others snapping pictures and talking loudly. Clergy dressed in a variety of ornate vestments strode through the crowds, immersed in a complicated set of rituals that didn't appear to involve anyone but themselves.

While the building has been destroyed and re-built several times, the current structure dates back to the twelfth century. Through the years it's been the focus of much strife—the First Crusade from 1096 to 1099, in fact, was partly sparked by this church falling under Muslim control. Even under Christian rule, the holy site has been plagued by discord. Since the thirteenth century, two Muslim families have been in charge of opening and shutting its doors each day, for example, because of so many squabbles between the Armenian Apostolic, the Greek Orthodox, and the Roman Catholics who have primary jurisdiction over different parts of the sanctuary.

The Church of the Holy Sepulchre is among the most peculiar holy sites I've ever visited. It's best described not as a church, but rather as a series of shrines. Inside the door, visitors climb the stairs to Golgotha, a spot marked with a gilded and highly ornamented Greek Orthodox altar. Descending the stairs, they pass by the Stone of Unction, which commemorates the spot where Jesus' dead body was anointed and wrapped for the grave, and then pass to the sepulchre itself, the spot where Jesus is said to have lain before his resurrection. Along the way are dozens of other shrines, ranging from the Chapel of Adam (where Adam's skull is buried, if one is in a credulous mood) to a place believed to mark the spot where Jesus met Mary Magdalene after exiting the tomb. Both somber and festive, magnificent and shabby, the Church of the Holy Sepulchre is an Old Curiosity Shop of the Holy.

As I approached the sepulcher, my heart sank when I saw the long line of people waiting to enter it. Debating whether I wanted to spend at least a half hour in line, I wrestled with my frustration at the crowds and the hubbub. Here I was at one of the holiest places in all of Christendom, and all I could think about was how much my feet hurt and how great it would be to take a shower. When Christian mystics like St. Francis of Assisi talk about identifying with the suffering of Jesus, I didn't think this is what they had in mind.

Tired and discouraged, I turned away from the shrine and headed to another part of the church, away from the crowds to a spot that I recalled from our tour the previous day: an unadorned room empty except for a somewhat decrepit altar. To one side was the entrance to a cave hewn out of rock, a space so small that a person could barely fit within it. Inside the darkness of the grotto, a small lamp was burning.

"According to tradition, this cave is the tomb of Joseph of Arimathea," our guide had said the previous day. "All the crowds go to the sepulchre, but I think this spot may well have been the place where Jesus' body was laid."

I didn't care much whether the guide's surmise was true. It was quiet there, for one thing, the noise of the crowds in the main sanctuary nearly inaudible. And I was mesmerized by the oil lamp that burned inside the cave, a light that created a halo of radiance in the shadows. It made me think of a line from the opening verses of the Gospel of John: "The light shines in the darkness, and the darkness has not overcome it."

It's not surprising that candles are used in rituals in nearly all faiths. With a simple strike of a match, they create an opening for the holy to enter—and the darker the surroundings, the more powerful the light appears to be. A candle, like many tools of the sacred, becomes most valuable to us when the way is obscured.

Seeing that flickering light, I realized that resurrection was far more likely to happen here than in the midst of the crowds in the main church. Like seeds germinating below ground, rebirth needs darkness and quiet. Perhaps it's a good thing that the rest of the world is so loud and busy that these places of resurrection get nearly forgotten.

I watched the candle for a long time before finally walking out of the room, through the church, and out into the crowded alleyways of the Old City once again.

Jesus Slept Here, Almost Certainly

The majority of Jesus' life was spent not in Jerusalem, but in Galilee, the agricultural region in northern Israel to which we headed next. In his day it would have taken about four days of walking to get from Galilee to the holy city; today it's a journey of just a couple of hours by car.

Because Jerusalem and its environs are dry and rocky, I was surprised by the lushness of Galilee. Partly this was due to recent rains, but our guide said that Galilee has always been the greenest and most fertile part of Israel.

We know very little about the life of Jesus before his public ministry began around the age of 30. The word used to describe his occupation was *tekton*, a term that can be translated as either a carpenter or, more broadly, a craftsman. His home village was Nazareth, which during his lifetime was a small place indeed, perhaps only about the size of two football fields. To the residents of Jerusalem, Galilee was a backwater, with its own distinctive accent to boot—think of how New Yorkers view people from the rural South and you'll have some idea of their attitude.

Then, as now, the Sea of Galilee was the jewel of the region. Contrary to its name, it's actually a freshwater lake fed by the Jordan River. Thirteen miles long and seven miles wide, the lake has hot sulfur springs near its southern edge, mineral-rich pools to which the sick have flocked for millennia. Some scholars speculate that the large number of sick people healed by Jesus were in the area because they wanted to take advantage of these healing springs.

Galilee made up for my mixed reactions to Jerusalem, as I loved its forested hills, green pastures, and groves of gnarled olive trees. I was especially taken by the lakeshore town of Capernaum, where much of Jesus' early public ministry took place. In the first century, Capernaum was far more important economically and politically than Nazareth. Surrounded by productive farmland and with abundant fish in the Sea of Galilee, it was connected to the rest of the country by an important trade route known as the Via Maris.

Jesus called his first disciples here: Peter, Andrew, James, and John, who were all fishermen on the Sea of Galilee, and Matthew, who was a tax collector (you probably wouldn't think of an IRS agent as disciple material, but Jesus did, despite the fact that in his day tax collectors were infamous for their corruption). In addition to preaching, the Gospels tell of him performing many miracles in the area, including curing Peter's mother-in-law of a fever, and bringing a child back to life.

Despite the groups of other tourists earnestly following their guides like ducklings, I found Capernaum to be a peaceful place, especially when I was able to snatch a few minutes to myself on the shore of the Sea of Galilee. I watched its waves lap the rocks, hearing the warbling of birds and the occasional chiming of a church bell. After the crowds and sensory overload of Jerusalem, this spot cooled by a breeze off the lake felt heavenly—the Holy Land, indeed.

My reverie ended when a friend called me back to our group and we walked to a nearby site that by tradition is identified as the House of Peter, whose first-century ruins were discovered beneath a fifth-century Byzantine church. We peered down through the glass floor of the church to the stones below, and I wondered if Peter, first a fisherman and then a fisher-of-men, really had lived here. Many holy sites in Israel have a hint of George-Washington-slept-here.

A short distance away, another spot was far more evocative: a fourth-century synagogue made of white limestone, with graceful, ornamented pillars. Our guide explained that below the present structure were the remains of a first-century synagogue, which is where many scholars believe Jesus preached. And a thought struck me. While I'd known intellectually that Jesus had been a real person, it hadn't really sunk in until I stood in that synagogue. And I had to ask myself, What did I actually think of this first-century carpenter?

Some Christians have a deep bond with Jesus and some don't. The man comes with a lot of baggage, though it's not his fault. I'd heard many people speak with such certainty about who he was, announcing with passionate assurance a wide range of contradictory beliefs. He died for our sins. He was a great teacher but nothing more. He was a political revolutionary or a crusader for social justice. He was a mystic, a healer, an avatar. He never existed but instead was constructed out of bits and pieces of ancient mystery cults mixed in with Greek philosophy. The Apostle Paul made him up.

Being in Israel forced me to stop putting Jesus into any single category, because the whole country is so complicated and its history so convoluted that I knew I could spend a lifetime there and still be at a loss. Some pilgrimage destinations trigger not certainty or understanding, but ever-greater enigmas.

At the same time, I felt like I knew Jesus much better after seeing where he'd lived, sort of like when you go home with a college roommate for the first time and you think, "Oh, *that's* why she's the way she is." I knew why he talked about goats and sheep so much, and that when he spoke about mother hens protecting their chicks, it was because he'd observed them in village yards many times. I knew that he'd also stood, like me, on the Sea of Galilee on warm afternoons and closed his eyes to savor the feel of a cool breeze off the water.

I couldn't identify much with the Jesus of the Temple Mount in Jerusalem, but I felt like I was beginning to better understand the one who'd walked the green hills of Galilee.

Another memory stands out from my trip to Israel. We were touring Bet She'an, an archeological site south of the Sea of Galilee that preserves the remains of a Roman-Byzantine city. At one point I turned away from the guide's description of Roman public baths and looked over the surrounding hills. I saw a few sheep coming over a rise, and then a shepherd came into view, walking with a long staff, followed by many more sheep. They followed him closely, grazing as they walked but always keeping their attention on him.

That single image has remained with me long after many of the memories of my journey have faded. It was a scene that has changed little in 2,000 years. Something about how those sheep responded to the shepherd, how they looked at him with perfect trust that he would safely lead them, made me realize that the Good Shepherd isn't just a cliché. It's an icon, a window into heaven, and it captures something of the essence of this man who intrigues and perplexes and compels me into often-reluctant belief.

Before coming to Israel, I'd recited the 23rd Psalm hundreds of times. But after that trip, it was never the same for me again. Sitting in a pew at All Saints, I'd hear its opening words, "The Lord is my shepherd," and I'd immediately be taken back, transported to that scene, watching as the shepherd led his flock over the crest of the hill at Bet She'an.

Library of Celsus in Ephesus, Turkey

CHAPTER 6

THE MYSTICS AND MARY

Theologians may quarrel, but the mystics of
the world speak the same language.

Meister Eckhart

~ PILGRIMAGE ~
The Temple of Artemis and House of the Virgin Mary
in Ephesus, Turkey

The Episcopal Church gave me an entirely new toolbox for being
spiritual. The liturgical range of this denomination is broad, meaning that if you're a High Church Anglican, there's not much difference between what you do on a Sunday morning and a Vatican mass.
If you're Low Church, your service has a lot in common with how the
Methodists are worshipping down the street. All Saints was somewhere
in the middle, with bells and smells—Episcopal-speak for the ringing
of bells and use of incense during the Eucharist—used mainly for special occasions.

As a convert, it felt to me as if a fascinating new set of people had moved into my neighborhood: the saints. I don't recall much emphasis on saints while growing up Lutheran, other than a few vague allusions to people who were exceptionally holy. Their piety provided models to aspire to, but the Catholics were misguided (no surprise here) in their devotion to them. All those statues and medals and thingama-bobs hanging from the rearview mirror were superstition, and also in bad taste.

But now, I delighted in being introduced to the saints. I loved how there's one for nearly every circumstance in life, from Francis de Sales, patron saint of writers and journalists, to Monica, patron saint of moth-ers, and Agnes of Rome, who watches over the Girl Scouts. Wolves have a patron saint (Peter), as do funeral directors (Joseph of Arimathea). In a particularly fine example of ecclesiastical irony, there's even a patron saint for enemies of religion: Sebastian.

I appreciated, too, how these people got to be saints not because they were perfect, but because they loved God with such extravagant fervor. Many of them started out on the wrong side of the tracks—thieves, bigamists, prostitutes, even murderers—but something made them turn their lives around and dedicate themselves to God.

I made friends with Teresa of Avila, who had ecstatic visions but who was also down-to-earth and tart-of-tongue. "If this is how you treat your friends," she once told God, "it's no wonder you have so few of them." I bonded with St. Patrick, who converted all of Ireland through his charm and respect for the native customs of the Celts. If a well or high hill was sacred to them, Patrick simply Christianized it. I can see him standing by a spring, saying, "Y'all think this is holy? Well, Jesus thinks so too!"

I could never predict what these saints would do with the crummy hands they'd been dealt by life. The sixteenth-century Spanish friar St.

John of the Cross, for example, had a perfectly miserable life. Though he was eventually named a saint, he was first accused of being a heretic, thrown into jail, beaten, and nearly starved to death. In prison, instead of hating his captors like any normal person, he wrote one of Christianity's most exquisite spiritual texts, *The Dark Night of the Soul*, which has been an inspiration for countless seekers ever since.

I learned that you didn't have to do grand things to become a saint, as the life of Thérèse of Lisieux, nicknamed The Little Flower, shows. Born in 1873 in France, at the age of 15 she entered the local Carmelite convent, where she died of tuberculosis nine years later. While early in her life she had a sentimentalized piety, in her last years she experienced a deeply troubling aridity of spirit ("Jesus isn't doing much to keep the conversation going," she said of her prayer life). In her suffering she turned to what she termed the "little way" of spirituality, seeking holiness in the ordinary, trusting like a child in the goodness of divine mercy. Virtually unknown at her death, Thérèse left behind a memoir, *The Story of a Soul*, that's been translated into more than fifty languages.

The saints I most admired were also mystics, which is one of those slippery words that's hard to define. But let me give it a try. Let's say you're setting out on a spiritual path and you come to a fork in the road. One fork is marked "Rationality," and if you go down that path you'll come to a library, where a bunch of philosophers and theologians are sitting around a big table discussing antinomianism, hermeneutics, eschatology, and modalistic monarchianism. Periodically they'll break for coffee. In the evening, take-out sandwiches will be served.

If you go down the other fork, labeled "Mysticism," you'll soon run into fog. You're going to get lost and scared, until some luminous creature points the way. You'll see the sky open and the clouds part and there's a good chance your entire body will be enveloped in fire. You'll attend the best party you've ever been to, one that lasts forever. Eventually you'll realize that none of this actually happened, but it doesn't matter because it's all true in some deeper sense that you can never explain to anyone.

The good news is that both of these roads end up in the same place, if you're a pilgrim guided by love.

The mystic path has often been viewed with skepticism by those who like their religion neatly ordered. An old joke in theological circles goes like this: mysticism begins in *mist*, centers on *I*, and ends in *schism*. I'll admit, when mysticism goes bad, it goes very bad (think doomsday cults). And it can be troublesome even when it goes just a little wonky— for example, your irritating neighbor with the flowing scarves and rock-solid assurance she's channeling wisdom from an ascended master.

I found an invaluable guide to the mystic road in the philosopher and psychologist William James. *The Varieties of Religious Experience*, a book he published in 1902, describes the four main characteristics of non-rational spiritual experiences: they're ineffable, meaning they can't be fully described in words; they give knowledge and insights that carry the weight of authority; they're fleeting; and the people who experience them do so in a passive state, meaning that while they can make themselves ready through rituals and practices, the mystical state comes and goes of its own accord. Writes James: "The mystic feels as if his own will were in abeyance, and indeed sometimes as if he were grasped and held by a superior power."

The Varieties of Religious Experience has made generations of readers feel depressed about the dullness of their lives. James writes about well-known mystics—visionaries like Teresa of Avila, Ignatius Loyola, John Bunyan, and Walt Whitman—as well as ordinary people who are often just going about their business when the mystic light breaks through.

Take, for example, this account from 1901 written by Dr. R. M. Bucke, a Canadian psychiatrist:

> All at once, without warning of any kind, I found myself wrapped in a flame-colored cloud. For an instant I thought of fire, an immense conflagration somewhere close by in that great city; the next, I knew that the fire was within myself. Directly afterward there came upon me a sense of exultation, of immense joyousness accompanied or immediately followed by an intellectual illumination impossible to describe. Among other things, I did not merely come to believe, but I saw that the universe is not composed of dead matter, but is, on the contrary, a living Presence; I became conscious in myself of eternal life. . . . The vision lasted a few seconds and was gone; but the memory of it and the sense of the reality of what it taught has remained during the quarter of a century which has since elapsed.

I'll have whatever they're having, thank you very much.

My fascination with mysticism infected Bob, and for a number of years we led what we called the Mystics Book Club, which included a wonderfully odd assortment of believers, eccentrics, and gadflies. We read many of the classics of mysticism, some of which were impenetrable, like the aptly named medieval treatise *Cloud of Unknowing*, and others that taught us that the mystic path is found in nearly all religions. I loved Martin Buber's *Tales of the Hasidim* and the *Tao Te Ching*, which is attributed to the sixth-century sage Lao Tzu, as well as the transcendent poetry of Jalal al-Din Muhammad Rumi, a thirteenth-century Sufi.

But my most unexpected education came, of all places, during a church meeting at All Saints. I don't recall the topic—I think it might have been a discussion of plans for an upcoming confirmation service or something similarly unremarkable—but I remember the story told by a woman in her late 80s sitting across the table from me. She was good-hearted and friendly, but she'd never struck me as particularly spiritual, until she said, apropos of nothing, "I was driving across the bridge near City Park last week when the most amazing thing happened. Suddenly everything was filled with light and I had this incredible sense of joy and peace. It probably lasted for just a couple of seconds, but I think it was the best experience of my entire life."

She smiled at us. There was a long silence, and then someone brought up the next item on the agenda. I appeared to be the only one struck by her words. I looked at her, sitting there in her matronly dress and orthopedic shoes, and I realized that her face was still radiant with the reflected glow of what had happened to her as she crossed the City Park bridge.

Mary Pops Up Again

It's pretty easy to trace a connection between my early years as a Wiccan with my devotion to the Virgin Mary. I'm not alone in making that leap, since many historians believe that the pre-Christian traditions of female deities morphed into the elevation of the mother of Jesus from a supporting player in the Gospels to a near-divine figure herself.

I was an unlikely convert to the Virgin Mary's team. When I was growing up, she belonged to the Catholics, except during the Christmas season, of course. Later, in my 20s, I accepted the standard feminist critique of her, which says that she perpetuates the patriarchal view that women should be either virgins or mothers (Mary being both, ta-da!). She was seen as submissive, obedient, and so idealized as to be worthless as a role model.

And then there's the doctrine of the virgin birth, which is an embarrassment for many Christians of a liberal bent. I once gave a sermon about the Virgin Mary in which I talked about how much I value her as an icon of both tenderness and strength. Afterwards a parishioner came up to chide me.

"We shouldn't be paying much attention to Mary," she said. "She symbolizes all the wrong things. And that stuff about the virgin birth is just ridiculous."

Well. *Pardon me* for bringing up a little detail that just happens to be one of the foundational doctrines of Christianity. (I'm so rarely orthodox in my theology that I have to take full advantage of being self-righteous when the occasion arises.)

Some biblical scholars trace the doctrine of the virgin birth to a translation error of a passage in Isaiah, which says that a young woman will bear a child as a sign of God's favor. "Young woman" was translated incorrectly as "virgin," leading to confusion ever since. I've had this explained to me so many times that I want to stick my head in a bucket every time someone tries to enlighten my ignorance.

Let me counter with this well-developed argument: I don't care. I put the virgin birth, along with most church doctrines, into the realm of poetry (my time as a Wiccan taught me this approach to theology). Many truths are best understood in this way. For example, I can say with utter conviction that my love is a red, red rose, but that doesn't mean Bob is a giant flower. The virgin birth works with similar layers of metaphorical complexity. I think the message has to do with the divine entering the world in a way that's both ordinary and extraordinary. It's the story of a woman who needed no man to serve as her intermediary to God. Fierce in her innocence, she sings a song called the Magnificat. "My soul magnifies the Lord," she begins, and then she proclaims that the mighty are being cast down from their thrones, the proud scattered in their conceit, and the lowly lifted up.

She may or may not be a virgin. But she's certainly no pushover.

Once Mary was on my radar, she began appearing everywhere. I saw her portrayed in paintings, depicted in statues, and clipped to the sun visors of cars. I read articles about people finding her image in the bark of trees, in water stains on the side of buildings, and in the burnt parts of a piece of toast. I often spotted her on lawns, hands outstretched near the peony bushes. She never appeared flustered or upset by being left outside in the rain, but instead seemed happy to have the chance to confer blessings on the grass, the flowers, and any dog that happened to trot by.

In my travels, I kept bumping into the Virgin Mary as well, because every corner of the world has a shrine dedicated to her. Through the centuries she's popped up in more than 2,000 places, and that's only counting the ones that got significant publicity. If she appears in a manner that's deemed authentic by the Church, another Our Lady gets added to her long list of titles, which include Our Lady of Loreto, Our Lady of Guadalupe, Our Lady of Walsingham, Our Lady of Knock, Our Lady of Manaoag, Our Lady of Chartres, and Our Lady of Fatima. Other titles she's picked up describe her spiritual qualities rather than her choice of real estate: Bride of Heaven, the Throne of Wisdom, She Who Shows the Way, Refuge of Sinners, Mother of Mercy, Joy of the Just, Mother of Sorrows, Queen of Heaven, Mother of the Poor, Queen of Confessors, and even Mary Untier of Knots.

While I'd once found Eastern Orthodox icons to be intimidating and strange, I was now drawn to the ones of Mary as *Theotokos*, Greek for "God-bearer." I was struck by how many of them have an undercurrent of sadness, as if Mary knows that the child in her arms will bring her great pain as well as joy. Seeing them often brought tears to my eyes, at the same time flooding my heart with warmth.

As my sons grew from toddlers to teenagers, Mary was my companion. I looked to her for guidance through the hard times of parenting, when I didn't know what to do other than pray. Most of all, I've relied on her to protect my children. Owen's illness seared in me the knowledge that I couldn't protect them from all harm. It wasn't that I didn't trust Jesus, but I knew that Mary had much more on-the-ground experience with children. She knew how to birth a baby, keep up with a toddler, remain sane with a teenager in the house, and keep the faith even as her adult child struggled.

She'd seen it all. And she was a good listener.

A Goddess, a Virgin, and Me

Of the many Mary shrines I've visited, my favorite is the House of the Virgin Mary near Ephesus, Turkey—though before I got to her home, I first needed to pay my respects to the Goddess Artemis.

I traveled to Ephesus with my friend Marian, who'd lived in Turkey three decades before and was eager to return. "Of course, we'll go to Ephesus," she told me when we were planning our trip. "You'll be amazed—everyone is awestruck at Ephesus."

The history of Ephesus stretches back to the Bronze Age, though the ruins visible today are remnants of a city founded by Lysimachus, Alexander the Great's successor. Later, Ephesus became part of the Roman Empire, growing into one of the largest and wealthiest cities in the world. A busy port on the Mediterranean Sea, it had a population of more than 200,000.

Ephesus was famous throughout the Greco-Roman world for being the site of the Temple of Artemis, one of the seven wonders of the ancient world. While Artemis was the Greek goddess of hunting, in this part of the world she became blended with other female deities of Asia Minor, particularly Cybele, an earth mother goddess of great power and influence. The Amazons, the race of warrior women, were said to have constructed the first shrine in Ephesus to this goddess. Over the centuries her temple was rebuilt several times, each time larger and grander than before. Its final incarnation was a marble structure four times larger than the Parthenon in Athens, with 127 columns 60 feet in height.

Inside the temple was her statue—and what a statue! It wasn't one of those classical Greek statues, the ones we still admire for their graceful beauty, but instead a Near-Eastern, highly symbolic representation of a female form. She had rounded lumps covering her torso, perhaps representing breasts, though some scholars speculate they're eggs, or perhaps the testicles of sacrificed bulls.

The thousands of pilgrims who came to worship at the Temple of Artemis helped make Ephesus a cosmopolitan city. It was a place of festivals, athletic competitions, theater performances, and processions through the streets—a blend of New Orleans and Paris, but with people wearing tunics and sandals.

Imagine being a resident of Ephesus during its golden age. You live in one of the largest cities in the Mediterranean world, a place protected by a powerful deity who attracts a steady stream of worshippers from distant lands. Ships fill its port, grand entertainments are staged in its amphitheater, and its marble buildings gleam in the bright sunlight.

Those who came to pay homage to Artemis likely thought that her power would continue forever. Because how can a deity die?

❧❧

Despite its splendor and wealth, Ephesus was not treated kindly by fate. The city was destroyed by the Goths in the third century, rebuilt by the Emperor Constantine, and destroyed again by an earthquake in 614. Many of the marble blocks from its homes and temples were carted off to make other buildings; the rest were left in disarray. As a final indignity, even its connection to the sea was lost when its harbor silted in. By the fifteenth century, the site was completely abandoned.

Archeological excavations at Ephesus began in the nineteenth century and continue to this day. Only a fraction of its buildings have been uncovered and restored, but even so Ephesus is one of the largest and best-preserved of all Roman-era cities. Millions of people visit its evocative ruins each year—including many Christian pilgrims, who come because of a man who arrived in Ephesus around the year 53.

When the Apostle Paul first came to the city, it was already home to a sizeable Jewish population as well as a small Christian community. Paul nurtured these new converts and worked tirelessly to make more, using the city as his base for about three years while traveling in Asia Minor as a missionary. While in Ephesus he wrote his *First Letter to the Corinthians*, the epistle that contains his often-quoted hymn to love, which begins, "If I speak in the tongues of men and of angels, but do not have love, I am only a resounding gong or a clanging cymbal."

To most residents of the city, however, Paul was just another itinerant religious crank. After awhile his passionate preaching stirred controversy in Ephesus, especially among the artisans who crafted miniature versions of Artemis and her temple for sale to pilgrims and tourists. When the silversmith Demetrius heard that a man in the city was saying that gods made by humans were not gods at all and should not be worshipped, he realized that his livelihood was at stake. He and his fellow artisans marched to the amphitheater shouting, "Great is Artemis of Ephesus!" They found some of Paul's followers, creating a scene that threatened to turn violent. A city official intervened and the mob dispersed, but Paul left the city soon after—not the first, nor the last, time the apostle found himself in hot water with the authorities.

Having read the Acts of the Apostles (the New Testament book that recounts this story) as well as other accounts of the glory of this ancient city, I was eager to tour Ephesus. But when I went through the entrance gate and saw just a few ruins I was disappointed. Oh, look at those broken columns—aren't they picturesque. And small.

Then I kept walking until I crested a hill and the panorama of Ephesus unfolded below me. That's the moment that made my heart leap, as I realized that Ephesus is still a Wonder of the World.

The sheer size of Ephesus is overwhelming. As I descended its main street, I passed the partially rebuilt ruins of one incredible marble structure after another—first a theater and temple, then a row of wealthy houses, then a brothel and bathhouse. I saw the remains of a marketplace were merchants had traded goods from around the Roman Empire and beyond. At the base of the hill stands the façade of a library that once was one of the largest in the world.

All of these treasures are set in a peaceful valley cradled by low-lying mountains, so that with even a little imagination, it wasn't hard at all to picture how it must have been in the days when pilgrims flocked to the Temple of Artemis and sailing ships filled the harbor. Ephesus is like a beautiful woman in advanced age, an echo of what she once was, but with a loveliness that shines through her bones.

The small details captivated me, from houses with mosaics that looked as new as if their owner had just stepped out to the market to buy olives and bread to streets with grooves made by chariot wheels. Along the central thoroughfare was an etched footprint directing sailors coming from the harbor to the brothel just up the street, proving that advertising isn't a modern invention.

The crown jewel of Ephesus is its amphitheater, little changed from the days when the followers of Artemis marched here in search of Paul. Its acoustics are still so fine that one can clearly hear the voices on the stage from the top row. I stood on that stage and looked upward at the rows upon rows of empty seats, once filled with 25,000 people. Those who came to Ephesus from afar must have been dazzled by what they saw performed here.

But amid this aged grandeur, there was one discordant note: the Temple of Artemis. Located in a marshy area a short distance away from the ruins of Ephesus, all that remains of that magnificent structure are just a few broken-down columns and a pool of stagnant water. I walked through the tumble of stones and tried to reconcile what I was seeing with its former glory. The forlorn remnants of the temple struck me as immeasurably sad.

Those who think their way of worshipping will endure forever would do well to visit this place haunted by the ghosts of pilgrims. Artemis, once a deity venerated by millions, doesn't live here any more.

⌘

As the worship of Artemis faded, Ephesus became a center for the new Christian faith. One strand of early church tradition says that the Apostle John settled here and that he wrote the Gospel of John in Ephesus. His remains are said to be buried under the ruins of the Basilica of St. John. And it's beyond dispute that the city became such an important Christian community that it was chosen as the site of the Third Ecumenical Council in 431.

Of all the Christian sites in the region, I was most eager to see the House of the Virgin Mary, where some say she spent her final years after moving here with the Apostle John. I knew that two stories are told about Mary: one that she died in Jerusalem and the other that she breathed her last at Ephesus. Barring some dramatic archeological discovery, we'll never know for certain if either is correct. But the foundations of this house may date back to the first century, and its general location fits with an early Christian tradition about the site of her home. As added evidence, in the early nineteenth century a German nun had a vision that Mary had lived in this exact spot, and who can argue with the logic of a mystical vision?

Part of what I appreciated about the House of the Virgin Mary is that there wasn't much there. In contrast to the throngs of people at Lourdes, there were so few visitors that I could hear the birds singing in the surrounding trees. Inside the small stone structure, a statue of Mary sat atop an altar, with two flickering candles on either side. In the space before the altar were two places to kneel and pray.

The house made me want to be still and silent—a sure sign that I'm on holy ground. And I sensed that this shrine was connected to the temple that once stood in the valley below. Whether the divine feminine is cast as a Mother Goddess, or as the Mother of God, the prayers are much the same.

As I knelt at the altar, I could imagine Mary living in that small house. After all she'd seen and suffered in her life, I hoped she'd ended her earthly days in a serene sanctuary like this, pondering in her heart all that she'd witnessed.

I was moved, too, when I exited the house and saw a small Muslim shrine to Mary. Our guide in Istanbul had told me that Mary is mentioned more often in the Quran than in the New Testament. "We honor her as Maryam, the mother of the prophet Jesus," he had explained.

As I watched, a group of women in headdresses and robes approached the shrine. I wondered what prayers they were saying as they paused there with closed eyes, and I knew that Mary made no distinction between those prayed by Christians and which by Muslims.

I thought of Mary sitting in that little house near the end of her life, sharing her story with those fascinated by the son she'd raised. "This is how it all began, many years ago," she says. "I was a young girl who had the most amazing thing happen to me." And then she tells them of the song she sang, there at the very beginning, and of angels and shepherds and kings showing up unannounced. From the perspective of long years, surely her song about the humble being exalted and the exalted humbled must resonate for her in a way it hadn't at the time she first sang it.

"My soul magnified the Lord," she says. "It still does."

❧

When our son Carl was in college, he spent a semester studying in Leuven, Belgium. Before he left, I made him promise that whenever he saw a picture or statue of the Virgin Mary, he was supposed to think of me—which was quite devious, because I knew that as a largely Catholic country, Belgium would have many images of her.

When I visited him late in his semester there, I learned just how effective my admonition was. There was not only a 50-foot statue of the Virgin Mary standing on a hill overlooking Leuven, but also a stained glass window depicting her above the door to Carl's dormitory. "You're pretty much in her sight everywhere you go, aren't you?" I asked him.

"You mothers don't miss a trick," he said.

That's correct. It's one of the reasons I'm so fond of the Virgin Mary. She shows up when she's needed, gathering us into her protective arms. But if we're not in trouble, she's perfectly content to wait on the sidelines, casting blessings our way whether we're aware of them or not.

Some truths are so large that only a myth can contain them. The Virgin Mary is one of them.

Abbey of Gethsemani in Kentucky

CHAPTER 7

FOLLOWING A CALL

In one sense we are always traveling, and traveling
as if we did not know where we were going.
In another sense we have already arrived.
We cannot arrive at the perfect possession of God in this
life, and that is why we are traveling and in darkness. But
we already possess Him by grace, and therefore, in that
sense, we have arrived and are dwelling in the light.
But oh! How far have I to go to find You in
Whom I have already arrived!

Thomas Merton

~ PILGRIMAGE ~
With Thomas Merton in Kentucky

Even though Thomas Merton had died decades before my visit, when I arrived at the Abbey of Gethsemani in Kentucky I somehow expected to see him striding down its paths. It seemed impossible that he was no longer present in this place that played such a key role in his writings.

At the abbey, I sought to better understand a man who's profoundly influenced my spiritual path, perhaps more than any other mentor. His call to religious life inspired my own—and of the two of us, it's difficult to say who was more surprised to end up on God's doorstep.

Merton was born in France in 1915 to parents who were artists. His American mother died when he was six and his father, a native of New Zealand, when he was fifteen. Merton received most of his education at boarding schools in England and France, lived in the U.S. for a time, and traveled widely, becoming a thoroughly worldly and sophisticated young man with little interest in religious matters.

But on a trip to Rome at the age of 18, he unexpectedly found himself drawn to churches. While he didn't participate in their services, he became fascinated by the art they contained, particularly Byzantine mosaics. "I began to haunt the churches where they were to be found . . . and thus without knowing anything about it I became a pilgrim," he later wrote.

This curiosity faded once he started at Cambridge University, where he enjoyed an exuberant social life, so much so that he lost the chance to return the second year. Merton returned to the U.S. and enrolled at Columbia University in New York, where his passion for writing and literature blossomed. He eventually earned his master's degree, writing his thesis on the English mystical poet William Blake.

Merton's interest in writing was accompanied by a deepening spiritual quest, and in 1938 he was baptized into the Roman Catholic Church. He applied to join a Franciscan order, but was turned down because of his youthful indiscretions, which may have included fathering an illegitimate child.

During a year of teaching at St. Bonaventure University in New York, Merton realized that his call to a monastic vocation could not be denied. After spending a retreat at the Abbey of Our Lady of

Gethsemani near Bardstown, Kentucky, he was accepted as a postulant there in 1941.

This is the point in the story where Merton should disappear from the world, for Gethsemani was not just a monastery, but a *Trappist* monastery. Known formally as the Cistercians of the Strict Observance, this order has strict commitments to the disciplines of silence and contemplation. Idle talk is discouraged and communication greatly restricted. The Trappist life is highly regimented and demanding, even by monastic standards—they're the Marines of the religious world.

If we could see Merton standing at the entrance to the abbey on that December day, we'd probably think, "Well, *this* isn't going to last very long." The twenty-six-year-old Merton just wasn't monk material: he was witty and engaging, a lover of jazz and literature, with leftish political leanings and a checkered past. And the world he was entering was practically medieval, with monks plowing the fields with horses, sleeping in dormitories with no central heating, and waking at 2:00 a.m. for a day that included seven prayer services.

But the call that Merton was hearing was as loud as a jet engine. With the zeal of a convert, he was prepared to give up everything for God—even his writing, his other great passion in life.

His abbot, thankfully, had other ideas. Intrigued by the new novice's unusual path to the monastery, he encouraged Merton to write his autobiography, a project that eventually became *The Seven Storey Mountain*. When the book was published in 1948, it became an unlikely, immediate success, selling 600,000 copies its first year and millions in the years since. In post-war America, it spoke to many who were searching for meaning in an increasingly materialistic society.

Merton went on to write poems, articles, essays, and more than 60 books, among them *New Seeds of Contemplation, The Sign of Jonas, Conjectures of a Guilty Bystander,* and *No Man Is An Island.* His publishing success greatly improved the fortunes of the Abbey of Gethsemani, as Merton's books brought in royalties and attracted novices drawn by his descriptions of monastic life (I know—waking up at 2:00 a.m. doesn't sound very appealing, but it takes all kinds).

I've considerable sympathy for the succession of abbots who directed the abbey during Thomas Merton's years there. Father Louis—as Merton was known within the monastery walls—must have sorely tried their patience at times. While he was an unusual novice, he became an even more unusual monk.

In Merton's early years at Gethsemani, he struggled with the sense that another monastery might be a better fit for him. And throughout his time there, he experienced tension between his desire for solitude and his love for human company. For years he asked for permission to have his own hermitage in the woods, a request his abbot finally granted in 1965. While the simple cinderblock house allowed him greater time for prayer and writing, he continued to meet with a steady stream of visitors. There's a paradox in all of this, of course. One of the famous criticisms of Merton was that he wanted to be a hermit just so long as his hermitage was in Times Square with a neon sign above it announcing, "Hermit lives here!"

Merton's wide-ranging reading, disciplined life of meditation and prayer, and connections with other spiritual leaders across the world helped his faith to deepen and change. In *The Seven Storey Mountain*, he'd written that he entered the monastery so that he could become closer to God. As he matured, he came to realize that a seeker can find God anywhere. One of his greatest insights is that all of us can be contemplatives, even if we don't wear long robes and live inside the confines of a monastery. He defined the path to be followed this way:

Contemplation is the highest expression of man's intellectual and spiritual life. It is that life itself, fully awake, fully active, fully aware that it is alive. It is spiritual wonder. It is spontaneous awe at the sacredness of life, of being. It is a vivid realization of the fact that life and being in us proceed from an invisible, transcendent, and infinitely abundant source. Contemplation is above all, awareness of the reality of that source. It knows the Source, obscurely, inexplicably, but with a certitude that goes beyond reason and beyond simple faith. . . . It is a more profound depth of faith, a knowledge too deep to be grasped in images, in words, or even in clear concepts.

While that sounds like Buddhism, this understanding of contemplation actually has deep roots in Christianity, as Merton learned through his study of mystics such as Meister Eckhart, St. John of the Cross, Gregory of Nyssa, and the third-century Desert Fathers and Mothers of Egypt. His exploration of these and other religious traditions, particularly Zen Buddhism, made him realize that the non-rational, mystical path is found in many faiths.

As Merton's understanding of spirituality changed, so did his sense of what was required of him as a Christian. He came to see that his monastic vows did not absolve him of his larger duties in the world. He became a passionate advocate for peace and social justice, writing on the issues of war and pacifism, racism, civil rights, and the nuclear arms race. He directed his words not to his fellow monks, but to ordinary people hungry for spiritual direction and guidance.

Merton died in 1968 of an accidental electrocution involving a fan while attending an interfaith conference of contemplative monks in Thailand. He was mourned by the people around the world who felt they knew him personally through his writings. Since then, his books, many of which have never gone out of print, have been translated into more than 30 languages.

I think the best summation of this remarkable man comes from the Fourteenth Dalai Lama. The two met in Dharamsala, India, shortly before Merton's death. They felt an immediate kinship, and even decades later, the Dalai Lama continues to refer to him in his public speeches. The most striking thing about Merton, he has said, was "the inner life he manifested. I could see he was a truly humble and deeply spiritual man. This was the first time I had been struck by such a feeling of spirituality in anyone who professed Christianity. . . . It was Merton who introduced me to the real meaning of the word 'Christian.'"

Merton, Living Still

Today Gethsemani is home to about 40 monks, who support themselves through farming and the making of fudge, fruitcake, and other handmade items, as well as the hosting of guests and royalties from Merton's books. (The Franciscans who turned down Merton's request to join their community probably feel like the editors who rejected J. K. Rowling's first *Harry Potter* manuscript.) The monastery honors its connection to its most famous resident but does not focus on it. Visitors can find information about him in a welcome center, but the mission of the monastery is prayer, not keeping the memory of a former monk alive.

The peacefulness of Gethsemani is palpable, both within the monastery walls and in the surrounding woodlands and rolling hills. Not much happens here, at least by secular standards. Continuing a tradition that dates back to the sixth century, the monks gather for prayer seven times a day, enfolding the cares and sufferings of the world as they follow an inner path of service rather than an outer one.

I actually liked the monastery church best between services. Spare and unadorned, it has two sets of pews facing each other for monks and another set of seats in the back for guests. Even its stained glass windows are muted in color and simple in style. Though my own tastes run more toward icons, statues, and rich colors, as I sat there in the empty church, its minimalist style began to speak to me. I started to notice subtle things, from the patterns the sunlight made as it crept along the walls to the way the silence came to feel like a living thing.

I recalled Merton's description of this church from *The Sign of Jonas*: "Even when I cannot think straight, God straightens me out as soon as I get a minute alone in church. It is good to go and pray even when you feel washed out. The mere effort makes you feel better. You are giving something of your silly self away, and that always nourishes you."

You are giving something of your silly self away—that's a marvelous line. And certainly this church, this haven filled with silence and sunlight, is a good place to let it go.

Sitting there, I thought of Thomas Merton's spiritual call as compared to my own, which felt a bit presumptuous, though I guessed he wouldn't mind, especially since I was there as a guest in his home. We were both unlikely converts who ended up on God's doorstep by meandering routes. We were rebellious at times, devout at others. We were Christians who were also deeply interested in other faiths. And we both struggled in our writing to put into words what cannot be expressed in words.

Outside the church, I paid my respects at Thomas Merton's grave, which is in the middle of the orderly, identical crosses of the monastery cemetery. The only thing distinguishing it from that of his fellow monks was a scarf tied around its cross. It appeared to be a *khata*, a white scarf associated with Tibetan Buddhism. I knew that these scarves are given as offerings when one comes before an honored teacher, their color signifying purity of heart and intention. The teacher then gives the scarf back to the student, as a token of blessing and an illustration of the karmic principle that giving and receiving are linked. It wasn't surprising to find such an offering there, for many Buddhists honor Merton as a fellow traveler.

I was happy to see that Merton is still making friends.

❧

As I walked away from the graveyard, I tried to shake off my introspective mood. I was headed to the office of the guest master. I was nervous, because even though I'd done hundreds of interviews, none of them had been with a Trappist monk. I worried that my conversation and questions would sound trite, since someone steeped in silence likely wasn't much for chit chat.

The monk who greeted me was dressed in a long white robe with an overlay of black cloth cinched at his waist with a belt. His face was serious but welcoming, and he gestured me with a smile to the seat in front of his desk. I pulled out my notebook and pen and asked my first question, one that I'd chosen with great care.

"What do you hope people will take with them from their time at Gethsemani?"

The monk leaned back in his chair and closed his eyes. Seconds passed. I could hear the clock ticking on the wall. More time passed. The clock ticked on. I wondered if he'd dozed off. I fiddled with my pen and notebook, looking at the other questions I'd jotted down. I knew I didn't have much time with the monk, and the seconds were stretching into minutes. I debated whether I should sneak out the door or wake him up.

Finally the monk opened his eyes and leaned forward. He obviously hadn't been napping after all. He answered my question with a single word: "Jesus."

I dutifully wrote down "Jesus" in my notebook.

Then there was more silence as I thought about what to do. Any question I could ask after that would surely be superfluous, for the monk's answer brilliantly summed up the entire reason to be in a monastery, either as a monk or as a guest. I thanked him and left, resisting the urge to tell him it was the shortest interview of my writing career.

I left the monastery by way of the church, standing once more in that soaring space filled with sunlight, pondering the monastic tradition that produced such men. It's not my spiritual path—I know I'm an exceptionally poor candidate for a cloister, despite my fascination with them. But I'm grateful such sanctuaries exist, places of silence and prayer that in some individuals can burn away the chaff, leaving wisdom behind.

❦

After departing Gethsemani, I had one more stop to make: the Thomas Merton Center at Bellarmine University in Louisville, an hour's drive to the north. During his years at the abbey, Merton had developed close friendships with several people at Bellarmine, and a year before his death, he named the school as the repository for his literary works and memorabilia. In 1969 Bellarmine established the center, which serves as an international resource for scholarship on Merton and his works and the ideas he promoted. With more than 50,000 items, it's the largest collection of his books, letters, journals, and photographs in the world.

I found its director, Paul M. Pearson, to be a chattier fellow than the guest master at the abbey. When I asked him why Merton continues to be so popular around the world, he answered with this: "He was an extraordinarily clear writer and thinker, which is certainly part of his appeal. But I think it's also that his work makes people feel as if they're reading their own thoughts, or maybe those of a best friend. He wrote so insightfully about spiritual matters and was so honest in sharing his own struggles. He was able to put people at ease, both in person and in his writing."

His greatest gift to the world, Pearson went on to say, is the way he integrated the paths of Mary and Martha. In the Gospels, Jesus visits these two sisters, one of whom was always busy with household tasks, while the other sat at Jesus' feet and listened intently to his words. "Merton didn't separate these two paths," said Pearson. "He felt that spirituality and action are linked and that you need both to be a whole person."

As I toured the center, I found it easier to get a sense for Thomas Merton the-man-and-writer than at the Abbey of Gethsemani. I saw watercolors done by his father, Owen Merton, as well as an exhibit of photographs taken by Merton, who inherited from his parents a love for artistic pursuits. I browsed books in which Merton had made marginal notes, their titles ranging across faiths and millennia, from Chinese philosophy and Sufism to Kafka and Hindu meditation.

I was intrigued by a display case that contained a selection of the few personal items Merton owned at his death. Inside were his monk's cowl, faded denim work shirt, eyeglasses, camera, and leather boots. It doesn't take much space to hold the worldly possessions of a monk.

What held my attention the longest was the manual typewriter that he'd used, a simple model from a pre-computer age. I was surprised that it wasn't protected behind glass. Glancing over my shoulder, not wanting to break the rules but finding the urge irresistible, I stood there for a few moments with my hands lightly touching the keys. It felt to me, standing there, that I received a blessing from my friend and mentor, long dead but living still.

When God Calls, Pick Up the Phone

After a decade at All Saints, I'd become so Episcopalian that not even a hint of my Wiccan/Unitarian slip showed underneath my skirt when I reached to the top shelf in the church's kitchen. Bob and I took our turns leading the prayers at services, coordinated adult forum on Sunday mornings, and knew where the extra chairs were kept and how to turn off the fire alarm if it was accidentally pulled. Our rowdy sons were now church broke—a process similar to breaking horses, only it doesn't include a saddle—and on Sundays we could usually sit with them through a service with our sanity intact.

I'd learned most of the arcane vocabulary of the Episcopal Church, which has rectors rather than pastors, sextons for janitors, and a vestry instead of a church council. For a year Bob served as Senior Warden of the Vestry, a title I thought should have included a hunting license and a blunderbuss, or at the very least the right to put misbehaving parishioners in stocks outside the church.

One of the Episcopal words that began to intrigue me was *deacon*, which, along with bishop and priest, is one of the three ordained orders of the church. While the roots of the Episcopal diaconate go back to the earliest years of Christianity, for many centuries the order largely disappeared as a separate entity and became instead a six-month interim on the path to becoming a priest. That changed in the 1970s, when the diaconate was revived as a separate, distinct order. Today deacons usually serve an Episcopal church on a volunteer basis and have some particular ministry as their focus, from working in prisons to helping refugees. They also have roles during the Eucharist, including reading the Gospel, assisting at the altar, and preaching.

While deacons typically don't attend a seminary, they go through a lengthy discernment process and training that culminates in a service of ordination. Unlike the ordinations you can get for $50 on the Internet, Episcopal ordinations are done by a bishop in fancy robes—even grander than the ones worn by priests—and a tall hat. And after that ceremony, deacons can wear a clerical collar, a fashion accessory that means everyone within earshot is going to try their best not to use swear words.

For more than a year, the thought kept reappearing that I might like to be ordained as a deacon. This is ridiculous, I kept telling myself. Having one low-paying job wasn't enough? Why would I want to take on one that was even less lucrative and that involved a lengthy process of preparation and jumping through many ecclesiastical hoops?

Despite my doubts, part of what attracted me to the diaconate was weariness from working alone for many years. My days were mostly spent in front of a computer, because while the research part of travel writing is fun, at some point I had to come home and write about all the places I'd visited. I found myself restless in a way that for me usually signals a change.

Being a deacon is in some ways like being a freelancer, in that deacons have considerable freedom to create a ministry that suits their interests and talents. I was intrigued by the possibility of preaching, too, because it was similar to the essay writing I enjoyed but with the bonus of a built-in audience. Even if people didn't like a sermon, they would dutifully sit through it, unlike in writing, where if I didn't capture their attention in the first paragraph they'd wander off. And I found it meaningful when people turned to me for a listening ear and comfort in hard times. It made me feel needed in a way that sending off a manuscript via email didn't.

I started a four-year Episcopal program called Education for Ministry, a study of the Bible, theology, and church history. While it was open to everyone, it was also, at the time, one of the prerequisites for ordination as a deacon. I didn't tell anyone but Bob about my ordination musings, because it was still too fresh and tender an idea.

In the midst of these deliberations, Bob and I and our boys spent a semester in the north of England. Bob had gotten a teaching stint at a college in Yorkshire, trading jobs with a woman who taught in the city of Bradford. We swapped houses and cars, with the English family living in our place in Iowa City, while we took over their home in the small town of Ilkley. Our boys went to an English school each day dressed in cute uniforms, and Bob and I learned how to drive on the opposite side of the road.

The semester was a wonderful experience, but not for the reasons we expected. The teaching wasn't particularly interesting to Bob, we found it hard to socialize with the reserved Brits, and it was a very wet and cold autumn, even by English standards. But what redeemed it all was the traveling we did on weekends and holidays. We focused, of course, on the holy sites scattered across Great Britain and Ireland.

Many of these sites are pre-Christian in origin, including standing stones, dolmens, and passage graves that date back many thousands of years. While Stonehenge is the most famous, such landmarks fill the British Isles. We didn't have to go far to find these prehistoric sites, because we lived in the shadow of Ilkley Moor, a hilly expanse of grass, heather, and bracken that contained hundreds of them.

While Bob was teaching and our boys were at school, I walked for miles nearly every day across the moor. I loved its brooding quality— just a few miles away, in fact, was Haworth, where the Brontë sisters had lived and gotten inspiration for *Wuthering Heights* and *Jane Eyre*. I delighted in searching out the many landmarks that hinted of ceremonial use by people who lived long ago, including rocks carved with intricate designs and standing stones arranged in circles. I didn't know why they were erected or what they meant, but I knew I loved sitting in the midst of those stones.

On the Sundays when we weren't traveling we went to a local Anglican church, which was picturesque, small, and attended almost exclusively by elderly people—the Church of England being, if not on its deathbed, at least wan and limping badly.

"Oh, you're back again?" some parishioner inquired nearly every Sunday, surprised that anyone but a dwindling English remnant would bother making the effort to attend church.

Those quiet services didn't give me much hope for the future of Anglicanism in England. But on my walks across Ilkely Moor, something was stirring. After we returned home to Iowa, I made the decision to seek ordination as a deacon in the Episcopal Church.

❧

When I was young and heard that our Lutheran church had called a pastor, I imagined that the call came directly from God, who used a special red phone that sits next to his desk in heaven. Later at All Saints, I learned that calls are indeed special things, even if they don't involve red phones. People seeking ordination dissect the nuances of their call before various committees, the equivalent of putting it under a microscope to see if it's legitimate. They talk to priests and bishops and take psychiatric examinations, all part of the process of distinguishing God's voice from an inner whisper that says, "Gee, I'd look really distinguished in a clerical collar."

But my time on pilgrimage with Thomas Merton taught me the most important characteristic of a call: from his example I knew that it has to be a living thing. If it's static, it dies, no matter how much it's watered with prayer and good intentions. Merton's call had first led him to renounce the world and enter a cloister, but then had brought him back into public engagement in a way that attracted controversy as well as praise. To the very end of his life he continued to change and grow as a Christian. He was never afraid to question his most basic assumptions or change his mind when he discovered his understanding was inadequate. The zealous young man who wrote *The Seven Storey Mountain* was very different from the contemplative monk who traveled through Asia on his final journey—just as I was very different from the young woman who thought she'd left Christianity behind forever.

I knew, too, that I'd already followed a variety of other calls in my life. I'd had a call to be a mother, a siren-like summons that hit in my late 20s when getting pregnant was the thing I wanted most in life. I'd felt a call to be a writer as well, a kind of persistent urging that kept me going through the ups and downs of freelancing. In some ways the call to ordination wasn't that different, except that it was public in a way that sometimes made me squirm. Having my innermost spiritual life opened up for inspection was a disconcerting experience. It was one thing to join a church; it was quite another to be so enthusiastic about it that you wanted to be up at the altar.

"So you think you're being called by . . . God?" asked a friend.

Seeing her expression, I recalled the days when I was the one who'd been skeptical of Christianity.

"Well, yes, sort of," I replied, witnessing to my faith with a bravery that I knew would not have impressed the martyrs. "I guess so. I think so. Most of the time."

Another friend was more blunt. "A deacon?" he asked. "How odd."

Part of it was the old-fashioned word *deacon*, which to many people brings to mind prune-faced puritans and pious do-gooders. I envied the cachet conferred by taking Buddhist vows, which also would have given me the option of wearing those graceful robes I'd long admired.

Bob was a mensch, as usual.

"Whatever you want to do, I'm behind you," he said. "Just don't expect me to play the organ or sing solos at church."

So for four years I put myself at the mercy of the ecclesiastical bureaucracy. I studied, wrote papers, passed a psychiatric evaluation, and sat in the All Saints basement discussing my innermost thoughts with members of a discernment committee. I went to Des Moines, where the bishop peered at me over his reading glasses as he inquired about my spiritual life. I was a little vague about my wanderings prior to returning to Christianity—the word "witch" does not come tripping off one's lips in a bishop's office—but I was honest about the fact that my path to ordination had been circuitous.

"Deacons are supposed to stand on the boundary between the Church and the world," I told him. "I'm comfortable there. And I think my varied background is an asset, not a liability."

The bishop approved my candidacy, and I was on the home stretch to ordination. And then, suddenly, I began to struggle with the idea that perhaps I was called to be a priest instead. Should I make religion my profession? God knows I was interested enough in spiritual matters. But I knew a career change would likely involve significant educational expense and upheaval in our lives, and I doubted whether I had the stomach to put up with parish life full-time, the dealing with budgets and committees and people's hurt feelings when they didn't get scheduled to serve at the Easter Vigil even though they'd been doing it for twenty years.

Most of all, I realized I wanted to remain at All Saints, which I knew wouldn't be possible if I became a priest. I'd grown to love my fellow parishioners. They were family, and I didn't want to leave them behind for another parish.

And so when the time came for me to stand at the altar in front of the bishop during my ordination service, I took a silent, personal vow: stability, which is a term I'd learned from the Benedictines. In addition to promising poverty, chastity, and obedience, monks and nuns in this tradition promise to remain in their community for life.

I certainly wasn't ready to pledge chastity. I wasn't a big fan of obedience. And though poverty comes naturally to a freelance writer, I was married to someone with a steady income. But something about *stability* greatly appealed to me. I'd wandered a lot, both in my travels and spiritually. Feeling like Thomas Merton standing at the entrance to the abbey on that December day in 1941, I was ready to commit to All Saints for the rest of my life.

St. Hildegard stained glass window in Bingen, Germany

CHAPTER 8

WISE WOMEN WISDOM

The marvels of God are not brought forth from one's self.
Rather, it is more like a chord, a sound that is played.
The tone does not come out of the chord itself, but rather,
through the touch of the musician.
I am, of course, the lyre and harp of God's kindness.

Hildegard of Bingen

~ PILGRIMAGE ~
Along the Rhine with Hildegard of Bingen in Germany

Ministry sounds so grand, doesn't it? This is one of the tricks churches play on their members, in fact, putting a shiny gloss on something that's just work-without-pay. Make it sound important and people are more likely to do it.

And yet, nearly every religious tradition recognizes that service is the royal road to spiritual transformation. Sitting on your cushion feeling holy is one thing; getting callouses on your hands is another. Putting your faith into action can make you feel like Sisyphus pushing a rock up a hill over and over, but something about the tremendous effort and frustration are essential to growth.

After I was ordained, it felt natural to focus my volunteer work in the church on healing ministry. Owen's illness had planted a seed that grew in my many visits to healing shrines around the world. And I found great meaning in being with those who'd entered the Kingdom of the Sick, that twilight world where some linger for a short time and others for years.

The final impetus came in the form of Jackie, who showed up at All Saints on the same Sunday morning as our new rector, Mel. Slight, short, with white hair and a kindly manner, she looked like the sort of new member destined to serve on the altar guild.

Years later, I accused her of entering All Saints under false pretenses.

"We had no idea you were a radical," I said. "You came through the door in disguise."

Jackie lifted her chin and smiled. "I've always been known for my eccentricities," she said.

Jackie had moved to Iowa City to live with her sister, and was of an age when most people are winding down their lives. In many ways, Jackie was just getting started. Over the next dozen years she became my mentor, my friend, and my inspiration for how to live fully in the spirit.

Her childhood was far from ideal. She grew up in California, where her talented but troubled father was a screenwriter in the early years of the movie industry and her mother was a poet and maker of costumes for opera companies. The two of them married and divorced each other three times, and during her childhood Jackie attended 15 different schools.

I asked her once how she'd emerged from that chaos such a stable and happy person. "What do you mean?" she asked me with genuine surprise. "I had a wonderful childhood. It taught me to see change as an adventure. And when we were in foster care with a Mexican family I even learned Spanish."

Jackie's resiliency served her well through her long life. During World War II she was a Rosie the Riveter, working in a factory assembling military planes, after which she enlisted in the Women's Army Corps. While in the military she met her husband, Phil, and together they raised two sons, Charlie and Bill. The most painful chapter in Jackie's life was Charlie's death from multiple sclerosis after many years of illness. But once again Jackie wrestled something good from hardship, because her son's long illness helped launch her interest in complementary healing. She became trained in Healing Touch, a technique of channeling energy to support mind, body, and spirit.

Soon after she arrived at All Saints, Jackie started giving Healing Touch treatments to the staff and parishioners. Our new rector, Mel, was supportive because his wife had received Healing Touch when she was undergoing treatment for breast cancer. A few members were skeptical ("This thing that new woman is offering, that touch thing," one of them told me, "I hope she doesn't give people the impression she's doing anything real.") A turning point came after a long-time member, well-respected in the parish, started receiving Healing Touch treatments after being diagnosed with cancer.

"Jackie makes me feel better," she said. "Whatever she's doing works."

❧

Healing Touch is based on a theory that a universal life force flows through the human body. This energy is recognized by many traditional cultures around the world and goes by names that include *chi* in Chinese, *qi* in Japanese, and *prana* in Sanskrit. Healing Touch, developed by nurse Janet Mentgen and launched as a formal program in 1989, uses techniques to rebalance and support this energy. Today medical centers, nursing homes, and hospice and chaplaincy settings around the world offer it to patients. Research has found concrete physical benefits from Healing Touch: it can help lessen tension and anxiety, reduce the need for pain medication, increase the immune response, promote wound healing, and trigger a sense of relaxation in patients. And it has an additional benefit: no harmful side effects. In both medicine and religion, that's a huge advantage.

"Look, the worst that can happen is that nothing happens," I told Mel as we talked about setting up a Healing Touch program at All Saints.

A year after Jackie's arrival, All Saints sponsored its first Healing Touch Spiritual Ministry workshop, and then another, and another. A team of people was trained and we set up a room dedicated to Healing Touch. Once a month, we offered a clinic in the parish hall that was open to the community. Jackie told us later that this had been her plan all along.

As a newly ordained deacon, Healing Touch intrigued me from the first time Jackie mentioned it to me. Part of my interest came from a physiological quirk that I'd noticed years before: if I concentrated, I could usually make my hands grow warm. When Jackie talked about channeling energy through her hands, I wondered if I could do something similar.

Jackie gave me enthusiastic affirmation. "Lori, you're a natural healer—I can feel it," she told me, holding my hands in hers. "God has given you an incredible gift. Use it."

I felt a little less like an Exalted Chosen One after hearing Jackie give this same speech to dozens of other people, each of whom lit up at her words.

"O.K., Jackie, level with me," I finally asked her. "Is there *anyone* who's not chosen by God to be a healer?"

"Probably," she said. "I just haven't met them."

Chakras in a Church

I'm standing in a small room at All Saints, my hands lightly touching a woman lying before me on a massage table. Soothing music is playing and sunlight streams through a window that overlooks a courtyard filled with blooming plants and ornamental trees. The walls of the room have works of art from around the world, each carrying symbolic meaning: there's a quilt made by peasant women in Mexico depicting miracle stories, a cross from a Trappist monastery in Iowa, and an icon of Hildegard of Bingen, the twelfth-century German mystic and abbess renowned for her healing skills. Overlooking it all is a small statue of the Virgin Mary standing with outstretched hands, a sculpture I'd brought back from Lourdes. As I complete a Healing Touch session with the woman who's recently been diagnosed with cancer, it feels like all of these icons and images are helping me channel divine energy to help bring her back to wholeness.

This scene can be viewed through a variety of lenses. In one sense, what I'm doing is a natural human response to someone in pain—touch. Think of the way we place a hand on someone's arm when they're hurting, for example, or cuddle a crying baby close. Research shows that a simple touch can slow breathing, reduce blood pressure, and calm stress hormones. It's our first sense, developing early in the maturation of a fetus, and often the last sense to leave us as we're dying.

Looked at through another lens, my actions are entirely in synch with Christian teachings, for laying-on-of-hands for healing has been part of the Church for many centuries. In this worldview, the energy being channeled is God's grace and blessing, and as a Healing Touch practitioner I'm following one of the commands given by Jesus to his followers: Go forth in my name and heal.

Healing stories fill the Bible, from Elisha curing a leper to Jesus stopping a woman's hemorrhage and restoring sight to the blind. The early Christian churches sheltered and cared for the sick, which is part of why the new communities attracted so many converts. Later, during the Middle Ages, monasteries often functioned as hospitals, with monks skilled in herbal arts treating the poor. Only later did spirituality and medicine separate, with healing becoming the sole responsibility of people in white coats.

In my own small way, as I worked in the healing room at All Saints I was part of a revolution in medicine, because growing numbers of people are realizing that spirituality can play an essential role in helping those who are ill. When people's bodies suffer, so do their minds and souls—and standard medical care is often insufficient to give them what they need.

I became adept at shifting my Healing Touch vocabulary depending upon my audience. If those seeking healing weren't religious, I talked about energy centers and the mind/body connection. If they were Christians who didn't know a chakra from a chipmunk, I spoke about the power of prayer in healing and invited them to visualize God's blessings flowing into them during the session. It didn't make any difference what words I used—the process was the same.

As I became trained in Healing Touch, I found that I could indeed sense energy flowing through my hands, a warmth that felt like it originated from a source beyond me. I grew to love the process of standing in silence as I laid hands on someone seeking healing. Part of it was that after many years of trying unsuccessfully to meditate, I'd finally found a technique that helped me quiet my monkey mind. As I followed the sequence of a session, my mind would become calm and still, allowing me to focus on the person in front of me and the sensation of energy flowing through my hands.

This doesn't mean I was always in a contemplative mood when I did Healing Touch. In fact, I'd often show up for a session frazzled from having to interrupt my day to come to church. But almost always my time in that room left me feeling rejuvenated and at peace.

Word soon spread in the larger community that patients diagnosed with cancer should try Healing Touch at All Saints. A group of about 20 volunteers served a steady stream of people who sought Healing Touch as an adjunct to their medical care. One by one they came to our healing room, where practitioners channeled divine energy into bodies that had been operated upon, tested, probed, radiated, and flooded with chemicals.

"This is the one hour of the week when I feel like myself again," one woman told me. "Actually, I feel better than myself—I feel joyful and at peace."

Largely because of Jackie, All Saints launched a Healing Touch ministry that sponsored the training of dozens of Healing Touch practitioners, benefited hundreds of people in the community, and inspired other churches around the U.S. and in several other countries to establish similar programs. Jackie was there every step of the way, encouraging us, helping us, and teaching us. She was the catalyst, but unlike many charismatic leaders, she didn't insist on remaining in control.

Well into her 90s, Jackie was giving a dozen or so Healing Touch treatments a week to her neighbors in the community where she lived. People would show up at her door unannounced for a treatment, sometimes late in the evening while they were wearing their pajamas, because that way they were ready to hop right into bed after she'd worked on them.

Even as she became increasingly infirm, she found ways to heal. On visits to the doctor she connected with people in the waiting room, choosing to sit next to those who looked like they were in pain or suffering.

"What a beautiful sweater you're wearing!" she'd tell them, and then strike up a conversation that would lift the shadows on their faces, even for a short time.

As Jackie approached the end of her life, I came to realize that while she was a gifted healer who'd honed her art over many years, what she did wasn't about techniques and wasn't something that could be taught or learned in a classroom. What she did best was love people. Love poured forth from her, continuously, effortlessly, radiantly. She herself knew that Healing Touch was really about that love. She could talk your ear off about chakras and energy centers, but in the end she always came back to this: "It's not about you. It's about being a clear channel so God's energy can flow through you."

Being of service gave Jackie more joy than anything else in the world—and that's the final, and perhaps the most important, lesson she taught me. Through her tutelage, I came to realize that while I'd been a seeker for many years, I'd missed one of the most essential parts of the spiritual path—service to others. In the hundreds of sessions I did in the All Saints healing room, I was slowly being changed, as imperceptibly as a stone is shaped by flowing water.

A Charismatic Nun-of-all-Trades

During the semester that Carl spent in Belgium—the time when he was under the close supervision of the Virgin Mary—Bob and I were eager to visit him. But when I looked at a map and saw how close Leuven was to Bingen, Germany, I knew we needed to alter our planned itinerary to visit someone nearly as important to me: Hildegard of Bingen.

While All Saints had Jackie, Bingen had Hildegard.

An abbess, healer, writer, musician, visionary, counselor, preacher, linguist, naturalist, and poet—as well as an adviser to kings, bishops, and princes—Hildegard was a Renaissance woman before there even *was* a Renaissance. Born in 1098, the last of ten children in a noble family, as a young girl Hildegard was dedicated to the Church as a tithe, the traditional ten percent owed to God. At 14 she entered religious life, going to live with her older cousin, Jutta, in a nun's hermitage attached to a male Benedictine monastery at Disibodenberg.

Jutta was a stern and ascetic sort, and I wonder how a bright spirit like Hildegard fared in such a constrained atmosphere. The two lived quiet lives, shaped by the rhythms of prayer, liturgy, and Bible study. While Hildegard didn't have a formal education, the Benedictines had great respect for learning, so she received instruction in natural history as well as religious matters, learning a rough-and-ready Latin that served her well in her later writings.

Hildegard grew into a learned woman interested in a wide range of subjects that went far beyond the cloister. She was also sickly, suffering from periodic fevers, pain, and fatigue. And she had a secret unknown to virtually everyone: she'd been seeing mystical visions from the time she was three.

At 42, Hildegard's life changed forever when she received a divine command to share these visions with the world. She described it this way:

> I am merely a too sensitive, frail rib with mystical lungs, who saw a living, blazing fire that couldn't be put out. . . . This Light said to me, "Shame-filled, earth-shod woman—untaught and unlettered—remember you've been illuminated by My light. It ignites in you an inner sun, burning with divine mysteries and secrets. Don't be timid. Tell these. Although you're hesitant to speak out, don't be. Speak of the Fire this vision has shown you."

By this time, Hildegard was the abbess of a small community of nuns that had formed at Disibodenberg. She spent the next ten years writing *Scivias*, a theological work that attempts to explain the blazing images she'd seen. With characteristic Hildegard chutzpah, she sent a draft of the manuscript to one of the most prominent religious figures of the day, Bernard of Clairvaux. He in turn sent it to Pope Eugenius III. And while popes throughout history have gotten many things wrong (for example, Galileo), this pope got it right. He declared Hildegard's visions to be divinely inspired, and from that point on the obscure German nun was launched into public life, gradually gaining fame and influence in both the religious and political realms.

At the age of 49, Hildegard founded her first abbey at Bingen, taking 18 nuns with her over the objections of the monks at Disibodenberg (Hildegard became ill when they refused her request, and then experienced a miraculous recovery when they relented). While Disibodenberg was in the hinterlands, Bingen was on the Rhine, one of the busiest travel routes through Europe. Though Hildegard was a nun, she liked to be where the action was.

During an age when women rarely lived into their 50s, Hildegard grew more creative and productive with each passing year. After she completed her first book, she started a second and then a third book of theology. She composed more than 70 songs for her nuns to sing, taking the standard plainchant of the day and turbo-charging it, greatly expanding its vocal range to create soaring melodies that one historian has described as the equivalent of Gothic cathedrals in music. She wrote books on medicine and natural history and corresponded with monks and nuns on spiritual matters and with royalty about political concerns, becoming a kind of Dear Abby of the Twelfth Century. She was both deeply mystical and roll-up-your-sleeves practical, a rare combination in any age.

At 60, Hildegard went on the first of four preaching tours, speaking in marketplaces because women were prohibited from speaking in churches. Seven years later she founded a second abbey on the other side of the Rhine because her own community had grown too large, crossing the river by boat twice a week to oversee it. And as if all of this indefatigable energy and creativity weren't enough, she even created her own language, a secret code that was discovered after her death. When she died at 81, they probably kept checking her body to make sure she didn't leap up for yet one more endeavor.

Here's Hildegard's own description of her life:

> There was once a king sitting on his throne. Around Him stood great and wonderfully beautiful columns ornamented with ivory, bearing the banners of the king with great honor. Then it pleased the king to raise a small feather from the ground, and he commanded it to fly. The feather flew, not because of anything in itself but because the air bore it along. Thus am I, a feather on the breath of God.

Healing, Visions, and a Strange Blue Man

The best way to arrive in Bingen is by boat from the north, because a slow journey through the verdant countryside of this stretch of the Rhine helps explain Hildegard's love for the natural world and her view of creation as holy.

Stepping off the boat, I smiled when I saw that the Hildegard Trail is marked by signs bearing the profile of a nun wearing a habit. (You don't see very many of those in the world of travel.) That trail led me first to the town's museum, where most exhibits are on Bingen's most famous citizen. I saw models of the monasteries where Hildegard lived, read excerpts from her letters and books, and studied displays on the daily life of a Benedictine nun during the Middle Ages. The ethereal, haunting background music, naturally, was composed by Hildegard.

I learned that during her day, the art of healing was mostly practiced by Benedictine monks and nuns. As an abbess, Hildegard treated both her fellow nuns and members of the larger community who came to her with complaints and symptoms. Like her contemporaries, she followed a form of medicine dating back to the ancient Greeks, who believed that four bodily fluids influenced people's temperament and health: black bile, yellow bile, phlegm, and blood.

Despite the peculiarities of this philosophy, Hildegard was also a strong advocate for many of the practices we've only recently re-discovered in Western medicine. She believed in the importance of a healthy diet, the value of moderation and rest, and the necessity of treating the entire person, not just their symptoms. She wrote extensively about the use of medicinal herbs, some of which are grown in the museum's garden. Above all, she knew people's physical and mental health is closely linked to their spirituality.

On the museum's upper level, exhibits focusing on Hildegard's mystical visions piqued my interest even more. Enlargements of them were arranged around a statue of Hildegard, each displayed in a lighted panel that allowed me to see their small details. Some were fiery and apocalyptic; others exuded a sense of serenity and peace. All were highly symbolic, which explained why Hildegard spent many years writing books trying to explain them.

Scholars believe that Hildegard did not create these images herself, but rather closely supervised their creation by scribes. They are some of the most vivid and complex religious visions ever recorded. After seeing them, I've even more respect for the ecclesiastical authorities who recognized them as divinely inspired, because these images would be easy to misinterpret. In her own time, some people thought her visions came from the devil, and without papal and church approval, her story might have been very different.

Her vision of the Trinity, which depicts Christ as a sapphire blue figure standing with palms facing outward, is one of her most famous. He's surrounded by concentric circles, the inner one of gold and the other of silver. Here is Hildegard's description of the image: "This is the perception of God's mysteries . . . that bright light bathes the whole of the glowing fire, and the glowing fire bathes the bright light; and the bright light and the glowing fire pour over the whole human figure, so that the three are one light in one power of potential."

Standing before this mesmerizing figure, I was struck by the position of Christ's hands: the palms seemed to radiate energy in a way instantly recognizable to any Healing Touch practitioner. It was as if all of the divine power of the Trinity poured forth from the hands of this strange, blue man.

❦

Still pondering what I'd seen, I made my way up the hill to St. Rochus Chapel, a church that illustrates the Lazarus-like nature of Hildegard's reputation. After her death in 1179, her memory was kept alive in this region of Germany but faded in the larger world. Then in the eighteenth and nineteenth centuries the German Romantics discovered her. With their love for the medieval era and close ties to the natural world, these poets and philosophers found a kindred spirit in the German nun. St. Rochus Chapel was constructed during this renaissance of interest. Neo-Gothic in style, it became a focus of devotion to her, with several of her relics (a.k.a. pieces of bone) kept in a treasure box.

Ornate panels near the altar illustrated scenes from her story, from her entrance into religious life as a young woman to her preaching tours around Germany as a mature and respected leader. Seeing them, I was reminded of the surprisingly large influence monks and nuns have had on history. Like Merton, Hildegard had expected to remain cloistered for the rest of her life, only to find herself interacting with the world in powerful ways. Some lights are too brilliant to remain hidden, even if they burn in out-of-the-way places.

After touring Bingen, I crossed the Rhine River by ferry to explore Hildegard's legacy in the town of Rüdesheim, where she founded her second convent when the Bingen abbey was full. Like her original abbey, this one was destroyed hundreds of years ago, but her legacy is flourishing at the Benedictine Abbey of St. Hildegard, which stands on a hill overlooking the towns of Rüdesheim and Bingen.

Surrounded by vineyards, the abbey was built between 1900-08, though it looks much older. During an era when Hildegard was largely unknown to the larger world, it was established to continue her spiritual legacy near the site of her original abbeys. While its overall design is neo-Romanesque, it features murals of Hildegard's life done in the Beuron style, which originated in Germany in the nineteenth century but draws on much older influences, particularly Egyptian art.

After the abbey was completed, a group of Benedictine nuns happily moved into their new home, honoring Hildegard's memory by singing her music, researching her history, and welcoming the trickle of guests who came on the Hildegard Trail.

That trickle began to swell in the 1970s and has been growing every since. Hildegard's life and achievements have been rediscovered by feminists, environmentalists, musicians, and artists as well as Christians, who each claim a different part of her life as a source of inspiration. For a woman who's been dead for eight centuries, her career is surprisingly robust.

Today thousands of pilgrims make their way to the Abbey of St. Hildegard each year, some for a brief visit and others for longer retreats. About 50 nuns live here, following the rhythms of Benedictine life that haven't changed much since the days of Hildegard. In addition to hosting retreats, the nuns have a variety of enterprises that support the community, including making wine from the vineyards that surround the abbey.

During my visit I was pleased to get the chance to visit with Sister Ancilla, who has been part of the community for more than 40 years. She told of how surprised the nuns were a number of years ago when Pope Benedict XVI mentioned *Saint* Hildegard in a speech. "We wrote to him and said that technically she wasn't a saint because she'd never been officially canonized," she said.

I can imagine the pope's chagrin—a mistake like this isn't good for the papal brand, especially given his German nationality. But once this omission surfaced, Hildegard was put on the fast track to sainthood with Teutonic efficiency. Pope Benedict named her a saint in May of 2012, and in October of that same year he designated her as a Doctor of the Church, an honor given to saints whose lives and teaching are deemed particularly important. Hildegard was only the fourth woman saint to be so honored, joining Teresa of Avila, Catherine of Siena, and Thérèse of Lisieux. At the Vatican ceremonies honoring Hildegard, the main image of her was taken from a mural at the Abbey of St. Hildegard.

"It took 800 years of prayer, but she finally was made a saint," Sister Ancilla told me with quiet satisfaction.

After leaving the abbey, I made my way down the hill to my final stop on the Hildegard Trail: the Parish and Pilgrim Church of St. Hildegard, which is also known as the Eibingen Church. It's built on the same spot where Hildegard's second abbey once stood. As I entered, my eyes were immediately drawn to the immense mosaic above the altar. Made of 150,000 small pieces of glass, it depicts Hildegard's famous vision of the Trinity, showing the figure of a blue man surrounded by two concentric circles, one of gold and one of silver. I've never seen a more unusual image on an altar.

Once again I sensed power radiating from Christ's hands, blessing those who come to this church in search of Hildegard. And I remembered this same image, much smaller, hanging in the healing room at All Saints. As I stood there, the two places and two eras became linked, separated in one sense by many centuries and thousands of miles, and in another by no time or distance at all.

❦

It's intriguing to think of the similarities between Jackie and Hildegard. Both were skilled healers who came into their full strength and influence as older women. Hildegard was 49 when she founded her first monastery; Jackie had been a wife and a mother for decades before finding her calling as a healer. They shared a love for artistic pursuits as well, with Hildegard producing an outpouring of creative works in various forms, while Jackie was a gifted visual artist and poet.

These two women taught me that weakness and tragedy can become the stimulus for spiritual growth. Hildegard suffered poor health her entire life, and it's likely that her struggles with illness helped spark her interest in healing. Jackie's passion for complementary medicine was shaped by her son's illness, and her suffering in losing him gifted her with the ability to respond to the pain of others with empathy and love.

A key concept in Hildegard's writings is *viriditas*, a word she used to describe the mysterious, divine vitality that fills the world. Jackie used a different vocabulary but had a similar understanding of the flow of energy through the world.

Most of all, the lives of these two women were infused with joy. Jackie's radiance was so powerful that I would tell people to sit next to her in church when they were feeling low, just so they could soak up her energy. And Hildegard's zest for life is expressed best in one of her famous sayings, a commandment that I think should be inscribed above the entrance to every church: "Be not lax in celebrating. Be not lazy in the festive service of God. Be ablaze with enthusiasm. Let us be an alive, burning offering before the altar of God." One of her mystical visions shows hundreds of angels circling around God in an endless dance of bliss, following her admonition.

Jackie died at the age of 96 (like Hildegard, she outlived the majority of her contemporaries). Hundreds of people came to her funeral, many of whom considered her one of their closest friends, even though they'd known her for only a short time. During the service, people were asked to stand who'd received a Healing Touch treatment from Jackie and just one or two people remained seated.

At the close of the service, Jackie's friend Chris led the congregation in the gospel hymn "I'll Fly Away." The sound of singing filled the church up to its rafters, with the chorus repeated again and again because people didn't want to it to stop.

I like to think that when Jackie entered heaven, she was greeted by Hildegard of Bingen.

Inca Trail to Machu Picchu

CHAPTER 9

IN THE VALLEY OF THE SHADOW

Learning how to hold sorrow close to our hearts is a spiritual practice,
a fierce and unflinching acknowledgement of the way of the world.

Francis Weller

~ PILGRIMAGE ~
Machu Picchu in Peru

I found it easy to form close bonds with the people I saw for Healing Touch, because I was meeting them at times of great vulnerability in their lives. Before we started a session, they'd talk about their struggles, from the trials of their medical treatments to their fears for the future. Often their illnesses became the catalyst for a reevaluation of their entire lives, leading them to deepen their ties with loved ones and make changes in their priorities.

What I heard in the healing room at All Saints made me think of the Jewish saying that God created humans because he loves stories. I loved hearing the stories, too, the tales of heartache and courage, estrangement and reconciliation. I was deeply moved by how people found meaning in their suffering. It was a privilege to be part of their healing journeys, even in a small way.

These stories helped illustrate a key principle of Healing Touch: the difference between a cure and healing. A cure is a cessation of the symptoms of illness—the broken leg is mended, the cancer goes into remission. Healing, in contrast, comes from the Old English word *haelen*, which means "to make whole." People's hearts and minds can be made whole even if their physical illness progresses. I saw this transformation happen many times during my years as a Healing Touch practitioner, especially for those whose diagnoses became terminal. For them, our sessions together became part of their preparation for death.

I came to think of the bonds I formed with people in the healing room as my Cherry Blossom Friendships. I was in Japan one spring during cherry blossom season, that brief period when a gauzy shroud of pink covers parks and gardens. Ordinary routines are forgotten when the trees bloom, with people picnicking and celebrating on blankets spread underneath the branches. The delicate blossoms symbolize the transitory nature of life, here today and fluttering to the ground tomorrow, a reminder of how beautiful, and how brief, existence is.

At All Saints, sometimes the healing room was full of cherry blossoms.

❧

I met Rich early in my tenure as a deacon at All Saints, shortly after I'd been ordained.

Rich and his wife, Sun Hee, were church shopping and had come to All Saints on the recommendation of a friend. They were an attractive couple in their mid-30s, vibrant and in love. I liked them immediately and enjoyed visiting with them at coffee hour. Rich told stories about his work as an elementary school teacher and Sun Hee, an artist who'd met Rich when he was teaching in South Korea, would talk about her latest sculpture project.

Within a month of coming to All Saints, their lives changed dramatically when Rich was diagnosed with a rare form of sinus cancer. Soon he began receiving Healing Touch treatments from me and a half dozen other practitioners as he started what would be a nine-year battle with cancer. While there were periods of remission, the advance of the cancer was inexorable, despite dozens of surgeries and hundreds of radiation and chemotherapy treatments. During the course of his illness, Rich endured more medical procedures and pain than any person I've ever known.

From Rich I learned the power of *agape*, a Biblical word that's hard to translate into English. The Greeks had a variety of terms to describe different types of love, from *eros*, love based on sexual attraction, to *phileo*, which describes a feeling of strong affection for something or someone. *Agape*, in contrast, was used to describe the love that binds God to humans and the members of a church community to each other. It's not based on warm feelings as much as action. You can tell if *agape* is present by how people act, not just by how they feel or what they say.

I came to appreciate having such a term to describe my love for Rich and Sun Hee, as our bonds were different than ordinary friendships. Once our connection was formed, there was no question that I'd be with them through the hard times—of which there were far too many.

I recall one of my last walks with Rich, just a week before his death. Once an athlete, by this time he was skeletal and weak, and each step he took down the hallway of the hospital required enormous effort. As Sun Hee and I supported him on either side, we slowly made our way around the nurses station. Rich had so little lung capacity that he could say only a few words.

"This is good," he said, then paused to take a few labored breaths. "It's good to be walking with you."

I've thought a lot about that walk, for it came to symbolize for me the tragedy of Rich's disease. During his youth Rich had hiked, biked, and roamed with a carefree sense of adventure, living in Venezuela and South Korea and touring many other countries. His dynamic, creative personality made him a natural teacher, and before his illness, he and Sun Hee had planned to make careers out of teaching in international schools. But in the last chapter of his life, his illness became his journey—not one chosen by him, but one that required every ounce of courage and strength he possessed. While I was traveling around the world seeking holy sites, he was making his own pilgrimage through hospital rooms, surgery centers, and chemotherapy infusion suites.

Despite his illness, Rich was a gregarious man who managed to lead a full life until nearly the very end. He loved his family, his students, and his wide network of friends with a passion that buoyed him through the harrowing cycles of treatments. Most of all, he kept fighting so he could live long enough that his young son Xavier (born after his first bout with cancer) would have lasting memories of him.

It's easy to idealize those who have died, but those of us who knew Rich well all have stories about his occasional orneriness. His personality filled any room he was in, and he was opinionated about nearly everything, from sports and politics to what should be included in a sermon. He could be stubborn and grumpy, especially when in the hospital, where he at various times complained about the food, the interpersonal skills of his doctors, how slowly nurses responded to his call light, the instability of the Internet connection, and the dust bunnies under the bed.

"Rich, you need to be careful or one of the nurses is going to smother you with a pillow," our mutual friend Lisa told him one day during a hospital visit. "And no one else will report her because they'll all be grateful."

To his credit, Rich burst out laughing.

Rich's irritability gave me one of my most important lessons in Healing Touch, though it was one I didn't appreciate at the time. I'd shown up to do a Healing Touch session with him at his house, where we kept a massage table because he found it difficult to get to the treatment room at All Saints. Bob had been there earlier in the day to help him put plastic on some windows in preparation for winter, and before we started the session, Rich told me about the poor job Bob had done. The plastic had wrinkles, he said. You could see them when you looked through the windows.

I was fighting my own irritation. Bob had spent several hours doing a job that Rich wasn't able to do alone, and Rich, instead of being grateful, was complaining about it. I knew he was sick and in pain, but I grumped through the session. I didn't pray or meditate. Instead of trying to channel healing energy, I mentally fussed.

At the end, Rich opened his eyes, smiled, and said, "Lori, that was amazing. Thank you so much. I feel much better."

It turns out that Jackie was right: as a practitioner, my job was to be a channel for God's healing, who apparently was able to love both Rich and me no matter how peevish we were.

Rich's intensity served him well in his passion for social justice. After college he was a teacher of inner city children at Amate House, a volunteer program for young adults run by the Catholic Archdiocese of Chicago, and throughout his life he volunteered for causes dear to him. In his last years, even as his health waned he worked on political campaigns, in particular the fight to help pass health care reform. "Anybody can land in the position I'm in, and no one should go through an ordeal like this without good insurance," he said.

During the re-election campaign of President Obama, Rich pushed himself far beyond the limits of what seemed humanly possible, knocking on doors, making calls, and taking people to the polls on election day. His efforts were so exceptional that he received an invitation to a Christmas party at the White House that year. One of my favorite photos is of Rich and Sun Hee standing at the entrance to the White House, Sun Hee leaning into Rich's shoulder, her arm around his waist, looking like she will never let him go.

In the Holy Land of the Hospital

Because I'd grown so close to Rich and his family, I was invited to be part of his last days, one of the strongest, hardest experiences of my life. While I'd visited many holy sites around the world, for those 48 hours, the palliative care unit at the hospital became the most sacred place on earth.

I was the last person Rich spoke to before his death. Sun Hee had called about 10 o'clock one evening, asking if I'd take him to the emergency room because of the terrible pain he was having. She'd stay with six-year-old Xavier, who was asleep. By that time there had been so many emergency room visits that the routine was familiar. I'd take Rich and she'd come to the hospital when she was able.

I picked him up and we started the drive across town. "Do you want to talk?" I asked him. Rich shook his head, his face white and drawn, his breathing harsh.

By the time we arrived at the emergency room, however, Rich's pain had eased considerably, as the medication he'd taken earlier took effect. For some reason I couldn't stop looking at his oxygen tank. During the past year I'd often seen him with this tank, but until I'd helped him carry it into the emergency room I hadn't realized its weight. It made me think of Jesus carrying his cross to the crucifixion, burdened by its heaviness. I hadn't known before, viscerally, what such a weight meant to a dying man.

We sat for an hour in the waiting room in companionable, tired silence. We'd been in many hospital rooms together, since I'd frequently accompanied him to appointments while Sun Hee stayed with Xavier. I wish I'd known then that it was the last time we would visit. I would have told him how much our friendship meant to me. I would have assured him that Bob and I would help Sun Hee and Xavier after his death. But I did tell him I loved him, and in the end, I guess that's all that matters.

Later that night, after he was given a bed in the emergency room, Rich's condition worsened. He slipped into unconsciousness and the attending doctor—who by a holy coincidence happened to be a friend of Rich—said that his family should be called, since he could die at any time. His mother Carol came from Dubuque, about a 90-minute drive, and Sun Hee brought Xavier, who was crying and bewildered from having been awakened from a sound sleep. It was 3 o'clock in the morning.

Carol, weeping, asked if I could do last rites. In the Episcopal tradition, this service of anointing can be said for anyone who is ill, but it's most often done for someone approaching death. I said yes, of course, then realized that in my hurry to get to the hospital I'd forgotten my small container of consecrated oil. Fortunately, the emergency room nurse had encountered this situation before.

"The security guard can let you into the chaplain's office—you can find anointing oil there," she said.

A couple of minutes later the guard and I were hurrying through the darkened hallways of the hospital, me praying all the while that I'd get back to Rich's room in time. When we reached the chaplain's office, I riffled through the desk and shelves with increasing urgency.

No luck. I couldn't find any oil. I said words that ordained people aren't supposed to say, especially when they're searching for holy oil. Then I had an idea.

"Is the cafeteria open?"

And that's how I ended up giving Rich last rites with olive oil I'd gotten from the salad bar—a bit of unorthodoxy that Rich wouldn't have minded at all. We gathered around his bed, his physician friend, Chris, joining us, and I began the ancient service for those nearing death. The words from the *Book of Common Prayer* were polished and smooth from having been prayed so many times at the bedsides of the dying:

> As you are outwardly anointed with this holy oil, so may our heavenly Father grant you the inward anointing of the Holy Spirit. Of his great mercy, may he forgive you your sins, release you from suffering, and restore you to wholeness and strength. May he deliver you from all evil, preserve you in all goodness, and bring you to everlasting life; through Jesus Christ our Lord. Amen

I dipped my thumb in the oil and anointed Rich's forehead and hands as well as his feet that were swollen with edema. In the mysterious alchemy of the Spirit, the olive oil wasn't salad dressing any longer. I thought of all the ways in which Jesus had claimed whatever was at hand for sacramental use—bread, water, wine, even dirt he scooped up from the ground. It wasn't much of a challenge for him to make that olive oil holy.

❦

Rich didn't die that night—he clung to life for another day and a half, giving his sister Beth, brother Gary, and sister-in-law Katie time to arrive. We kept vigil by his side, supported by the attentive staff of the palliative care unit. As when Owen was ill, I'd entered a state in which time ceased to exist.

I looked at Rich's family and wondered how they could possibly survive this loss, which was coming just four months after the death from cancer of Rich's brother, Paul. I imagined losing my own two sons, especially so close together. My heart physically ached to see the distraught grief of Xavier, who was just starting to comprehend what was happening, and the desolation of Sun Hee, losing her beloved husband at such a young age. The pain they were experiencing was so raw, so powerful, that I can only describe my reaction as one of awe. This word has become cheapened by overuse, but its original meaning describes the overwhelming feeling of reverence or fear produced by being in the presence of power. That's what I felt, there in that hospital room, hour after hour.

In the waiting room I'd recalled the agonizing journey of Jesus to his death, weighed down by his cross. In that hospital room with Rich's family, the image that kept coming to my mind was of the women who gathered at the foot of the cross as Jesus was dying. They could do nothing to help him, but they remained there because their love for him was too strong to leave. All they could do was bear witness and wait. I felt entirely useless in Rich's room, too, except for being able to wait.

On the evening of the second day, as I made the sign of the cross on his forehead after saying the final words of the service for the dying from the *Book of Common Prayer*, Rich died. Despite having been unconscious for nearly 48 hours, it seemed he heard the words of release that I spoke. I felt a slight jerk of his head as the life force left his body, as if a cord had been cut. One moment he was alive, and the next his spirit was gone. And then there was a feeling of lightness and buoyancy in the room.

Earlier in the day, Rich's mother told a story about him as a toddler. When he was learning to walk, she said, each day he'd go to the front door and demand to be let outside, so they set up a snow fence in the front yard where he could play. But whenever Rich was put into the enclosure, he immediately went to its gate and cried to be let out. In the spring they put up a chain link fence around the entire yard—and then Rich would go to its front gate and still cry to be let out. For the rest of his childhood, she said, it was hard to rein him in.

When Rich died, it felt as if he'd been released from the final barrier that held him back. I had the deep, unshakeable sense that Rich had entered into joy, escaping a broken body that could no longer contain his indomitable spirit.

While Rich's suffering had ended, his family was now struggling to cope with the reality of his death. It was clearly time for Xavier to leave the hospital room, because he'd reached the limit of what a six-year-old can endure. "Should I take Xavier to the lounge?" I asked, knowing the answer even before they responded. I felt grateful for having something concrete to do.

A minute later we were walking hand-in-hand down the hallway. We found a comfortable chair in a TV lounge and I wrapped my arms around his small body, holding him close.

Remembering that time, it makes me think of how easy it is to get ordained ministry wrong. Too often we think that the most important thing clergy do is lead rituals and preach at an altar. But what is most significant can look quite commonplace. I felt like I was doing some of the most important ministry of my life, holding Xavier in my arms as both of us pretended to watch cartoons through our tears.

Memories in My Backpack

Three weeks after Rich's death, I left for Machu Picchu in Peru, which probably seems about as far as I could get from a hospital room in Iowa. But it turned out not to be so far at all.

A month before he died, Rich asked me where I'd be traveling next. When he learned I was making plans to visit Machu Picchu with a group of travel writers, a smile came across his gaunt face. "I loved Machu Picchu!" he said, and proceeded to tell me of his visit there when he was teaching in Venezuela in his 20s. He described the rigors of hiking the Inca Trail and how moved he was when he finally came through the Sun Gate to see Machu Picchu for the first time. Then he said this: "When you go there, take me with you."

His words hung in the air, for we both realized there were no more trips in Rich's future. But I told him that I would, knowing it would be in spirit only.

As I traveled in Peru, I kept in my backpack the program from Rich's funeral. It included a picture of a young and healthy Rich looking far different from the person I'd said goodbye to in that hospital room. I began to connect this Rich to the places I was visiting, and gradually, thoughts of his hard last years were replaced by a realization of the full life he'd enjoyed before his illness.

A kind of bifurcation of awareness happens when we travel with memories of a lost loved one. "I bet Rich loved this place," I thought as I wandered the aisles of the Cusco market, with its intoxicating blend of sights, smells, and sounds, from pig's heads hanging from hooks and baskets overflowing with pungent spices to the music of panpipes and drums played by street performers. I imagined Rich watching with pleasure the young children chasing pigeons in the central square in

Lima, and the lovers who strolled along the cliffs that overlook the ocean in the city's Miraflores district. Through this blending of memories, I realized that my friendship with him had changed, but not ended, with his death.

My experiences mirror those of many spiritual travelers, because pilgrimages are often undertaken after a loss of some kind. In the midst of grieving, the need to escape our ordinary routines can grow within us, an urgent call to seek healing in a new place. On the road, amid the rush of new sights and sounds and experiences, mourning can lose its bitter edge.

❧

The goal of my trip was Machu Picchu, but before I arrived at that legendary destination, I had a lot of learning to do. I knew I couldn't even begin to understand this mysterious site without some background on the Inca culture that created it.

My crash course in Peruvian history began at Lima's Larco Museum, where I discovered that *Inca* is a term for a ruler, similar to caesar or czar. The century-long Inca Empire had just 16 Incas, all members of a tribe that today is known as the Quechua, who still live in the Andean mountains.

"The Inca Empire was in control of Peru when the conquistadors arrived, so a lot was written about it by the Spanish," explained our guide. "That's the major reason it's so well-known. The empire actually spans just a small chapter in Peruvian history, which stretches back 5,000 years."

Beginning around 1440 CE, Inca rulers forged the New World's largest pre-Columbian empire, one that stretched from southern Colombia to central Chile and from the arid plains of coastal Peru to the Amazon jungles. They did so with a combination of ruthlessness, efficiency, and practicality. Tribes and cities that accepted their rule were incorporated peacefully into the empire. If they resisted, they were swiftly conquered. By the late-fifteenth century, the empire was a well-oiled bureaucratic machine. Powered by the labor of peasants and including some ten million people, it was wealthy and sophisticated. Roads connected the farthest reaches of the empire, linked by runners who carried messages between cities. Similar to the ancient Romans, the people of this civilization were masters of architecture, road-building, and civil administration.

Their greatest emperor was Pachacuti, whose name means "he who shakes the earth." Like all Inca rulers, he was considered a demi-god as well as a political leader. Through conquest and skillful leadership he created an empire composed of many different tribes and ethnicities, ruled by an elite. He built grand monuments and huge fortresses, including, most likely, Machu Picchu.

Then came an unexpected threat. Soon after Columbus landed in the Caribbean in 1492, the diseases of Europe began to filter south. Within a few years, smallpox had killed many natives, including Huayna Capac, the leader of the Inca Empire. A civil war followed, further weakening the society. By the time the Spanish conquistadors arrived, the kingdom was vulnerable and fragile.

On November 16, 1532, Francisco Pizarro and his band of 167 Spaniards met the emperor Atahualpa in the small Andean town of Cajamarca. Atahualpa was curious about the ragtag group of men and was particularly intrigued by their horses, an animal new to that region of the world. Although he'd already made plans to kill Pizarro and his men the next day, he foolishly allowed them to approach him—a decision that changed the course of history, for if Atahualpa had annihilated the Spaniards right then, things might have turned out very differently. Other conquistadors would have arrived, to be sure, but perhaps they wouldn't have been as ruthless as Pizarro.

But Atahualpa let his curiosity get the better of him. Pizarro seized the moment, attacking with a barrage of charging horses, blasting cannons, and gunfire, none of which the natives had encountered before. Within just a few hours, the Spaniards had killed thousands and captured the emperor.

Caught in a trap, Atahualpa made a generous bargain with Pizarro. In exchange for his life, he offered him a ransom that consisted of a large room filled with treasure three times over—once with gold, and twice with silver, a fairy tale sort of bargain. Over the next months, precious objects poured in from throughout the empire. As promised, the room was packed three times with the precious metals. But Pizarro reneged on the deal and killed Atahualpa anyway, thus sealing his reputation as one of the biggest S.O.B.s in history.

That tragedy was a foretaste of what would unfold over the next decades. The Spaniards staged a brutal take-over of the Inca Empire, greatly aided by their superior weapons and use of horses. While there was brutality on both sides, the invading Spaniards were far more savage. A remnant of the once-mighty empire staged a desperate guerrilla war against the invaders from the city of Vilcabamba in the Amazon region, but were finally conquered in 1572.

On my tour of Peru, I could see many ways in which the Inca Empire still influences its culture, despite having been defeated four centuries ago. Some Peruvian buildings, particularly in the former capital of Cusco, have Inca foundations. Builders shaped the huge stone blocks so precisely that they needed no mortar to hold them together, constructing buildings that have remained standing even during major earthquakes, unlike a good share of their modern counterparts.

Inca traditions also continue to shape the spirituality of the country. High in the Andes, in particular, people practice a mixture of Catholicism and much older beliefs. The Virgin Mary, for example, is frequently depicted in forms that recall Pachamama, the earth mother. To honor her, people pour a splash of whatever they're drinking on the ground before taking their own first sip. Other divine beings are honored as well, and many of the native peoples still believe that *apus*, or spirits, live in the mountain peaks—including at Machu Picchu, where I headed next.

The Sacred Web of Machu Picchu

In 1911, a Yale professor named Hiram Bingham made a discovery that catapulted him to international fame and put a remote site in the Peruvian Andes on the bucket list of generations of travelers. In his book *Lost City of the Incas*, Bingham describes the moment:

> Hardly had we left the hut and rounded the promontory than we were confronted with an unexpected sight, a great flight of beautifully constructed stone-faced terraces, perhaps a hundred of them, each hundreds of feet long and 10 feet high. . . . Suddenly I found myself confronted with the walls of ruined houses built of the finest quality Inca stone work. It was hard to see them for they were partly covered with trees and moss, the growth of centuries. . . . I could scarcely believe my senses as I examined the larger blocks in the lower course and estimated that they must weigh from ten to fifteen tons each. Would anyone believe what I had found?

Bingham in one sense didn't "discover" Machu Picchu—its location had long been known to those who lived nearby, as well as to a few Europeans who'd trekked through the surrounding jungle. But he brought the site to the world's attention, thanks to his Ivy League position and his association with *National Geographic Magazine*, which publicized his explorations in multiple articles. It also helped that Bingham had a gift for self-promotion and a substantial ego; in fact, he would later become the inspiration for the movie character Indiana Jones.

So what did Bingham find? The answer is complicated, because while much is known about Machu Picchu, many mysteries remain.

Machu Picchu was built in the fifteenth century during the glory years of the Inca Empire. Its physical location is dramatic, occupying a narrow promontory of land surrounded by mountain peaks and encircled on three sides by a loop of the Urubamba River. It's been called the world's most perfect blend of architectural and natural beauty.

The site's buildings fill much of the space between two peaks: Machu Picchu (which means "old peak" in Quechua) and Huayna Picchu (meaning "young peak"). About 60 percent of its structures are original, while the rest have been rebuilt. The hilltop settlement includes three main areas: a royal and sacred section, a secular quarter where workers lived, and more than 100 terraces where crops were grown. Machu Picchu is a marvel of civil engineering, linked by staircases and kept dry in the frequent rains of the cloud forest by an intricate drainage system.

One of the puzzles of the site is that it didn't have any obvious military or strategic use. Some scholars speculate that it was the equivalent of Camp David for the U.S. President—a royal retreat away from the Inca capital of Cusco, which lies 50 miles to the southeast. The site was occupied for only about a century and then was abandoned after the conquistadors took control of the empire. It was never discovered by the Spanish during the Colonial Era, and gradually was engulfed by vegetation.

I'm actually embarrassed by how little effort I expended to get to Machu Picchu. Before visiting, I had the idea that it's only reached by hacking through dense jungle. Instead, I took a bus and train from Cusco and then another bus to the promontory where Machu Picchu sits (though I must say that bus ride is plenty scary, with multiple hairpin turns and steep drop-offs). If I visit again I'll take the Inca Trail, the arduous hiking route that leads up and down the mountains before emerging at Machu Picchu. It felt like cheating to arrive there so easily.

But however you reach the site, the first full view of Machu Picchu has an impact that's physical in force. On the morning I visited, a light rain was falling and clouds swirled around the stone buildings and terraces cut into the steep hillsides like stairways for giants. It seemed impossible that human hands had built this huge settlement in such an isolated spot, especially without modern technology. I stood for awhile simply looking at the scene, hardly believing that it was real.

While the site below me already had hundreds of tourists scrambling up and down its trails, I suspected I wasn't the only pilgrim there that day, as Machu Picchu is one of the world's great holy sites.

Many scholars believe that Machu Picchu had spiritual significance from its very beginning. Its location was likely chosen in part because of its proximity to mountains and the Urubama River, which was considered sacred. Its plazas include multiple shrines, temples, and carved stones, some of which are oriented to astronomical events such as the winter and summer solstices and spring and fall equinoxes.

For example, a carved block of granite known as the Intihuatana is arguably the most sacred spot at Machu Picchu. Its name is Quechua for "the tether of the sun." The term refers to the theory that the stone was once used as a kind of astronomical calendar. At the spring and fall equinoxes, the stone casts virtually no shadow, leading to the theory that perhaps the people who lived here thought that the post somehow kept the sun from retreating farther from the earth.

For years tourists were allowed to place their hands on the Intihuatana. Now, unfortunately, it's roped off, so I can't report firsthand whether it's full of energy, as some New Age enthusiasts claim. But its position and careful shaping suggest that this stone was considered highly significant by its creators. Another indication is that similar stones found at other sacred sites in Peru were all damaged by the Spaniards, who obviously saw them as representing something important to the native people and thus a threat to their control.

I'm intrigued as well by a theory advanced by the scholar and explorer Johan Reinhard, who believes that for the people of the Inca Empire, Machu Picchu formed the sacred center of a huge area. It was the hub of a spiritual web, connected to other holy sites in the region and to celestial bodies in the sky, surrounded by deities who lived in the surrounding mountain peaks and the sacred river far below. As such, it was an important pilgrimage destination in the past, just as it is today.

Another image kept coming to my mind as I walked the steep trails of Machu Picchu. It felt like one of those thin places beloved by the Celts, a spot where the veil between heaven and earth is transparent. In exploring spiritual destinations around the world, I've never come across a better description for why certain places simply feel *different* from other sites. I think that's why Machu Picchu, despite its exotic setting, seemed familiar to me in some ways, for I sensed something there that I've experienced at other holy sites, from Lourdes and Ephesus to Galilee. It felt like coming home.

❧

For a couple of hours I wandered at random at Machu Picchu, listening to a guide at first, then exploring the site's twists and turns on my own. All the while I was looking for something, a quiet spot where I could sit undisturbed. By the time I found it, the rain had ended and the sun was peeking out from behind the clouds, bringing warmth to the chilly day. I settled into my out-of-the-way perch overlooking the mountains, took the program from Rich's funeral out of my backpack, and held it in my hands. I sat there for nearly an hour, feeling the sun's warmth on my face, watching the clouds swirl around the peaks while birds glided past, buoyed by updrafts from the valley below.

Sitting there, I came to suspect another reason why the Inca rulers had chosen to build in this spot. It was, perhaps, because the mountains demanded it. Something about them kept drawing my gaze. Maybe Machu Picchu was built at this spot to make it easy for people to sit as I was doing and gaze upon the peaks.

In Chinese Taoism, there's a long tradition of painting such landscapes, because it's believed that contemplating mountains, both in nature and in art, nurtures the spirit. I love the ways humans are incorporated into these paintings as tiny figures at the base of the rocks. They provide a sense of scale, showing the vastness of the crags in relation to humans, but there's also a kind of symbiosis that's created between the high elevations and the traveler, as if the two need each other to fully express their true natures.

There on the side of the mountain, I thought about that walk Rich, Sun Hee, and I had taken through the palliative care unit of the hospital. I realized that Rich's brief circuit around the nurses station had probably required as much determination and strength as the entire Inca Trail had years before.

And I had a sense, sitting there, of my own mortality. After decades of exploring, I was beginning to realize that my own journeys wouldn't go on forever. They may end swiftly through an accident, or slowly, as a result of illness or advanced age. It was now my turn to bask in the sunlight at Machu Picchu, but eventually I, too, would yield my seat at such places to other travelers.

The thought triggered an overwhelming sense of gratitude: for Rich's life and for my friendship with him. For the fact that when he was near death, he could still find happiness in his memories of places like this. For my own experiences of sacredness around the world.

Before I left that spot, I tore off the photo of Rich from the funeral program—the one that showed him young and healthy—and wedged it into a crack in the wall. Then I stood with my hand over the opening, saying a last goodbye to my friend, bidding him to keep watch over those holy mountains.

Rich was there with me at Machu Picchu, gliding with those birds, released at last from the body that could no longer contain him.

Bear Butte in South Dakota

CHAPTER 10

BECOMING A BEAR

Crucial to finding the way is this: there is no beginning or end.
You must make your own map.

Joy Harjo

~ PILGRIMAGE ~
Bear Butte in South Dakota

Among the chronicles of religious revelations, from Moses receiving the Ten Commandments on Mount Sinai to the Apostle Paul's vision on the road to Damascus, my insight that raccoons and bears are closely related doesn't seem like much. But this epiphany, which I had while camped at the base of Bear Butte in South Dakota, ranks as one of the most significant moments in my spiritual life, one that would set in motion a series of life-changing events.

As important truths often do, this insight snuck up on me without warning. I was, as the French put it, a woman of a certain age, with graying hair and a comfortable routine of family, friends, and work. My sons were young adults, well-launched in their own lives. I was a

Christian—a little unconventional in my theology, true, but a committed believer nonetheless. I was so involved at All Saints that I was practically part of the furniture.

And then, the Holy Spirit came upon me and said, "Let's think about this whole bear thing."

This shift in my life actually began at an adult education program on a Sunday morning at All Saints. As part of a series on spirituality and the addiction recovery movement, the speaker was Jim Stands, who lives on the Rosebud Indian Reservation in South Dakota. Jim told us about the history of the Lakota people, their complex and proud traditions, and the many ways in which they'd been unjustly treated since their first encounters with White settlers and the U.S. government. He told his personal story as well, including his struggles with alcoholism, the commitment to sobriety that saved his life, and his efforts to help his fellow Lakota through the recovery center he directs on the reservation.

Bob and I invited Jim to dinner that night, and over the meal we had a wide-ranging conversation about Lakota ways. Bob told him about being introduced to Indian traditions while growing up in South Dakota and about teaching classes in Native American philosophies at his college. We said we both felt a deep connection to the South Dakota landscape through our trips to visit Bob's family in the Black Hills. We felt especially drawn to Bear Butte, a peak just east of the Black Hills that's both a state park and a spiritual site for many Plains Indian tribes, including the Lakota and the Cheyenne.

Jim knew it well. "It's a holy place," he said. "I've been there many times for ceremonies."

Then he made us an offer we couldn't refuse: "The next time you go to South Dakota, stop by and see me."

A month later, we were driving around the Rosebud Indian Reservation with Jim and his friend, Sylvan White Hat. As we traveled down smooth highways and on rough gravel roads, through small settlements with names like Antelope and Swift Bear, past mile after mile of grasslands, we began to see the land through their eyes.

We learned that the 20,000 people who live here trace their lineage to the tribes of the Great Sioux Nation, which signed treaties with the U.S. government in the 1880s recognizing their rights as a sovereign government. The Sioux Nation includes seven tribes, one of which is the Lakota. Within that tribe, those who live on the Rosebud Reservation are the Sicangu. They continue to have the status of a sovereign nation, which gives them the right to manage tribal affairs, create and enforce tribal laws, elect officials, and regulate their own territory.

As we drove, I found the reservation beautiful beyond my expectations. I'd thought it would be more like the neighboring Pine Ridge Reservation, which is drier and harsher in its topography. Instead we saw many places that reminded me of the Black Hills, with valleys laced by streams and rivers, thick pastures where cattle and bison grazed, and sweeping vistas of sky and clouds.

Sylvan showed us around Sinte Gleske University, which offers a variety of arts and sciences and vocational degrees and where he'd taught Lakota language and culture classes in years past. We had dinner at the Rosebud Casino, one of the reservation's major employers. We learned of the efforts to educate the children in Lakota language and traditions and of the sun dances, sweat lodges, and pow wows held on the reservation. And we visited St. Francis Mission, a Jesuit ministry that sponsors a church, school, dental clinic, museum of Lakota culture, and radio station, as well as the recovery center that Jim directs.

There was much to admire on the Rosebud Reservation, but Jim also talked about its dysfunctions. Some of the towns we passed through were poor and bleak, with ramshackle houses and an air of defeat. Crosses were a frequent sight on the side of the roads, poignant reminders of the reservation's high rates of fatal accidents because of drunk driving.

"Nearly every social problem we have is directly tied to alcoholism and addictions," Jim said. "No program or intervention can help until people get sober. That's why the recovery movement is so important here."

I knew from Jim's presentation at All Saints that he is a devout Catholic, and I asked him how he integrated his Lakota spiritual traditions with his Christian beliefs. He said that in the past, reservation churches had been very resistant to native practices, but that his Catholic parish now welcomes those who follow Lakota spiritual ways as well as Christian ones.

Our conversation turned to the subject of spiritual connections to animals. The concept of animal helpers had long intrigued me, and I'd read many accounts of how cultures around the world believe that nature is alive with unseen forces and that humans can develop deep bonds of kinship with other species. I asked him how people could discover their spirit animal.

"The owl is my spirit," Jim said in response, not answering my question. And then he launched into a long story. He told of growing up in an Indian boarding school and of the many ways that system had been disastrous for native people, who were forced to give up their language and customs to take on white culture. He recounted his years of drinking, his troubles with the law, and his many damaged relationships.

All through these years, Jim had viewed owls with wariness and more than a little fear, for the Lakota associate these birds with both positive and negative powers. Medicine men can take their shape, so you can't be sure whether an owl is an animal or a person who may do you harm. They're said to have the power to herald a death and prophesy the future.

One of Jim's most significant encounters with an owl occurred when he was a young boy. One day when he and his brothers were playing in the woods, they came upon an owl sitting in a cottonwood tree, a rare sight since this species is usually active only at night. The owl didn't fly away even when they shouted at it. One of the boys picked up a stone and threw it at the bird, and soon all of them were throwing rocks.

"We were wild, ignorant kids, and we stoned the owl to death," Jim said.

Through the next decades of Jim's life, during his long years in the wilderness of alcoholism, owls kept appearing to him again and again, often at significant moments. After he entered recovery and began to rebuild his life, he came to recognize his spiritual connection to them, but he always remembered the terrible thing he'd done to one of his owl brothers as a boy, and it continued to trouble him.

"One of the Twelve Steps is to make amends for past wrongs," he said. "After I got sober, I went one by one to all the people I'd hurt. But how could I make amends to a dead owl?"

One day while driving, he saw the carcass of an owl lying on the side of the road, likely hit by a car. He got out of his vehicle and stood looking at it, mourning the beauty of its mottled brown and white feathers and its eyes clouded by death. He put the bird in his car and brought it to a medicine man so that its wings could be made into fans for ceremonial use. Then he took the rest of the body back to a place he recalled from long ago: the cottonwood tree on which the owl he'd killed had been sitting, many years before.

"I dug a grave for the owl underneath that tree," he said. "While I was digging, birds started to gather in the surrounding trees, and then they began to sing. I knew it was a death song for the owl. After I'd placed the bird in the ground and prayed over it, the birds left. And then I heard an owl call from a hill in the distance. I got in my car and searched for it, and found it perched on the branch of an oak tree. I sat for a long time looking at that owl. I felt like it was giving me a message that I'd been forgiven for the wrong I'd done to the Owl Nation."

He fell silent, his face pensive as he drove. I looked at him, this Lakota man who had told me so much about his life and his people's history in a single narrative.

"You honor me by telling me your story," I told him. "Thank you."

Jim nodded. "When you find your spirit animal, you'll know," he said.

Raccoons, Reconsidered

After visiting the reservation, Jim's story about the owl kept coming back to me, awakening a restlessness that I hadn't felt in many years.

For years I'd been leery of being just another white person appropriating Native American culture in a superficial way, akin to someone who does a weekend workshop in Sedona and passes himself off as a shaman. On the other hand, like many people who've spent significant time in wild places, I knew some powers and truths are best expressed in animal symbolism. The more attuned we are to the forces of nature, the more certain animals come to us in our dreams, meditations, and prayers, becoming allies and teachers if we welcome them.

On one of our family's summer camping trips to the Rocky Mountains, we sat around a campfire talking about wild animals we loved. Bob felt drawn to raptors, especially owls, Owen to mountain lions, and Carl to wolves. In one sense this was the sort of idle conversation people tend to have as evening falls and the flames flicker in the night, creating a cocoon of light surrounded by the shadows of the woods. But our discussion had a more serious side as well, as we analyzed characteristics that helped define us and pondered spiritual traits we hoped to invite into our lives.

As for me, I'd known for some time that a particular animal came up again and again for me at significant times in my life. It had brought Owen back to life again after nearly dying from meningitis and acted as a catalyst for insight for me at other times. The problem was that I was a little embarrassed by my animal affiliation.

"I'm afraid I'm a raccoon," I told my family. "We wash our food in streams and tip over garbage cans. We have cute little hands and black markings that make us look like Zorro." (No disrespect is intended to those who claim a kinship with raccoons.)

Given this background, I can see now that I was primed for my epiphany while camping at Bear Butte. A thunderstorm had passed through earlier in the afternoon, cooling the air and awakening the prairie flowers and birds into vibrant life. Bob and I spent the entire evening looking up at the mountain from across the small lake at its base, watching as the sunlight gradually faded and a full moon rose in the night sky. I could see the way the low-lying mountain resembled a sleeping bear, and I thought of how I'd love to have a bear as my animal. And then it came to me: "Bob, aren't raccoons related to bears on the evolutionary tree?"

"Hmmm," Bob said, making the sound he uses when I come up with some wild idea that he's not certain about but knows enough not to squelch. "You might be right."

I went to sleep that night thinking about the question. I'd always been an Iowa girl who lived far away from bears in their natural habitat. Perhaps the raccoons I'd encountered at key times in my life were actually emissaries from another species.

The next morning, Bob and I hiked Bear Butte, following the narrow, rocky path that leads to its top. We climbed separately, as we often did on the mountain, the better to focus on our own thoughts and prayers. And sitting on the side of Bear Butte, looking at the Black Hills in the distance, feeling the warm prairie wind against my face, it became clear to me that my animal was indeed the bear.

Jim was right. I knew. It was an identity that I hadn't been ready to claim before, but the time had come.

With the benefit of hindsight, I recognized that this truth had been hidden in plain sight for much of my life. I remembered coming to Bear Butte for the first time in my 20s, and how I was drawn to it again and again on our visits to the Black Hills. Even though the region has far more scenic hiking trails, this was the place to which I always wanted to return. Our treks there became a kind of pilgrimage before I even knew what a pilgrimage was. I recalled walking to its summit with a baby on my back, and how we later would have our boys stay with their grandparents so we could visit the mountain for our own private meditations without children in tow. I realized that Bear Butte, more than any other holy site, had inspired my passion for spiritual travels.

Sitting there, I pondered the symbolism of bears. I already knew of their intelligence and strength, their ability to hibernate through long winters, and their fierceness in protecting their cubs. But I'd never considered the ways in which I was like a bear—or, more precisely, how I *wanted* to have those qualities for myself. I came to see how over the years I'd grown less interested in pleasing others and more independent, more willing to stand up for what I believed despite what people thought of me.

Moved by these insights, I prayed that I might be worthy to claim the bear as a spirit guide. I don't recall how long this reverie lasted— probably not very long, but it was long enough. I walked slowly down the mountain, full of gratitude, delighting in the small flowers that lined the path and the way the wind danced with the grasses. I felt different, somehow, from when I'd climbed the path earlier that morning.

Entering the visitor center where I was to meet Bob, I saw a Lakota woman working behind the desk. Still trying to make sense of my revelation, I asked her what bears symbolized in Lakota culture.

"Bears?" she said. "Oh, bears are connected to healing. They're about healing of all kinds."

A Prairie Landmark Purified by Fire

The Lakota people call Bear Butte *Mato Paha*, Bear Mountain, a reference to the way its profile resembles a sleeping bear. Red Cloud, Crazy Horse, and Sitting Bull all visited this peak to pray, and it continues to be a place of vision quests, sweat lodges, and other ceremonies for Indians from throughout the United States and Canada.

It might be an overstatement to call Bear Butte a mountain, at least in terms of its physical stature. Formed from volcanic rock that's been worn into its present shape over millions of years, it's visible for miles across the prairie, but at 4,400 feet it isn't nearly as high as the peaks of the Black Hills.

Holy sites and recreation don't mix easily. At Bear Butte, government officials have attempted to deal with these difficulties by reserving part of the mountain for Indian ceremonial use. Non-native visitors can make the hour-long hike to the top of Bear Butte, but other areas are off limits. People are asked not to take photographs of any religious artifacts and be respectful of those who are there for spiritual purposes.

But even on the public trail to the top, it's clear this is holy ground. Ribbons of cloth and small bundles of tobacco (which is regarded as a sacred herb by Indians) adorn nearly every tree and bush. Many of the offerings are faded by the sun; others more recent. Sometimes on my hikes there I've heard the sound of drums from nearby ceremonies, a rhythmic counterpoint to my steps.

The mountain is nearly treeless because of a fire that swept over it in 1996, a blaze that destroyed ninety percent of its vegetation. For a time, blackened stumps covered its steep slopes, but by now most of these have fallen and are slowly returning to the earth. I remember what Bear Butte was like before the fire and am sometimes wistful for the beauty of the pine trees that once offered shelter and shade on hot summer days. But my sorrow at the devastation caused by the flames has gradually changed into a recognition of how the mountain now feels purified.

Because the peak is so exposed to the elements, the effects of the Dakota sun and nearly constant wind are amplified on Bear Butte. If you're looking for a pleasant afternoon hike, this isn't the place. Among the many outdoor attractions in the Black Hills, it doesn't get a great deal of publicity, and I'm sure some of its visitors leave disappointed. I've also heard of people who've had negative experiences there. One man climbed halfway to the top but then turned back because the mountain felt hostile to him. Another person I know also turned back, because he felt that as a non-Indian he'd no right to be there.

I've never felt unwelcome on Bear Butte, but I do have a keen sense that I'm a guest there. I don't fully understand its magnetic pull on my spirit. Certainly part of its attraction is that my annual visits have imbued it with personal significance: when I climb Bear Butte, I have the chance to reflect on the passage of time and the changes in my life since my last visit. Part of its sacredness, too, is due to the fact that so many people over the centuries have come here for spiritual inspiration, saying prayers that have seeped into its rocks and soil.

❧

Through our friendship with Jim on the Rosebud Reservation, on one of our visits to South Dakota we visited Bear Butte Lodge, an educational, spiritual, and cultural center located at the base of the mountain. Run by the Rosebud Sioux Tribe, it's open to everyone, but has a primary mission to host tribal events, groups, and individuals. Its caretaker is Corey Hairy Shirt, a Lakota man who welcomed Bob and me on a warm August day.

"Bear Butte has been a holy site for thousands of years," Corey told us. "Many tribes come here to pray and do ceremonies. Whites are welcome to come, too, but we hope they'll be respectful when they visit. Christians don't want someone coming into the middle of a church service playing a radio, but sometimes the equivalent of that happens on Bear Butte. That's why we try to teach non-Indians about what this holy mountain means to us. We want them to understand how we do things here."

In thinking back on our visit, I realize that Corey taught us about Bear Butte in a way entirely in keeping with Lakota tradition: he told us stories. He spoke first of his own life, of how he'd grown up on the nearby Rosebud Reservation and struggled for years with alcoholism before entering recovery at the age of 30. He told of moving back to the reservation to make amends to those he'd hurt and of reconnecting with his family, community, and Lakota traditions.

A key part of Corey's spiritual path has been the sun dance. For nearly 30 years, he's been participating in this ritual, first as a dancer and now as a ceremonial leader. While different tribes have their own variations of this religious ceremony, all forms of it require great physical endurance and courage. Corey explained that you don't dance for yourself, but as a sacrifice and prayer for your family and loved ones. "That first year, my mother had suffered a stroke and I decided to dance for her healing," he said. "People told me it would be the hardest thing

I'd ever done. You dance for four days with nothing to eat or drink, with the skin on your chest pierced and tied to a central pole. That first year, there was a time when I didn't think I could complete it, but I did."

Corey's mother lived another 17 years, and Corey kept dancing. Today he teaches others who wish to take up the sun dance tradition, while continuing to learn about its meanings himself.

As caretaker of the Bear Butte Lodge, Corey meets a wide variety of people. Some are well-versed in the mountain's history and traditions; some arrive unaware of what it represents. "This mountain has a life of its own, and it's different every day," he told us. "But there's something here that draws people, even those who don't know much about it. They're often surprised by the emotions it stirs up in them. I tell them, 'Remember where you're at—this is one of the best places in the world to come and pray.'"

While Corey believes it's important for non-Indians to have an understanding of what goes on at Bear Butte and other native holy sites, he, like many Indians, is wary of those who try to appropriate these traditions for their own, particularly those who charge money for ceremonies.

He told us a story that conveyed this point in an understated way. Several years ago he met a young man, a non-Indian, who was taking part in a sun dance as part of a paid workshop taught by someone based in California. When he asked the young man how long he'd prepared for the ceremony, he said three months. When he asked him where he'd gotten his pipe and other ceremonial objects, he said he'd purchased them. When he asked who he was dancing for, the young man said for himself, that he was struggling in his job and thought it might help.

Corey gently told him of his own path to the sacred circle, how the sun dance requires a year of preparation, how everything that's used in it must be made by or given to the dancer, and how the dance is done as a sacrifice for loved ones, not for yourself. He said that the requirements of the sun dance don't end after the ceremony is completed, for once you take up the sacred pipe, you can never put it down—from then on you have a responsibility to pray for your people.

"The next morning, the young man came to me with all of his things packed and said he was going home," Corey said. "He told me my story had made him realize that this wasn't his path, and he was grateful to me for teaching this lesson to him."

I came away from our meeting with Corey Hairy Shirt with a deep respect both for him and for all those who are carrying on native traditions at Bear Butte and on the neighboring reservations. They have the difficult task of maintaining a balance between guarding what is holy and welcoming all people of good will.

As we drove away from the mountain that day and I saw its outline silhouetted against the sky, I thought of Corey's story of how Bear Butte came to be. He said that many years ago, a terrible monster stalked the land. A bear came to protect the people and there was a battle between the two of them. The bear finally won and threw the monster south, where it landed in the Badlands. There you can still see the thorny ridges of its back sticking up from the ground. The bear, wounded and bleeding after the fight, laid down and died on this spot, his body forming what is now the holy mountain.

"Here the bear remains, still protecting its people," Corey told us.

After more than 30 years of visiting Bear Butte, I think this story is true—in all the ways that matter.

❧

When I told Jim about my epiphany on Bear Butte, he didn't seem surprised. "The mountain spoke to you," he said. "I've known many people who have a bear for their spirit animal. It's a powerful one to have."

183

I was struck by his matter-of-fact response, which indicated that there was nothing unusual in discovering my inner bear. And perhaps it wasn't peculiar at all, because for most of human history, this kind of connection was commonplace. You're an owl, I'm a bear, your mother is a wolf. At different times in your life, other animal spirits may appear to guide you. Remaining open to their wisdom is prudent, not foolish.

In the harsh light of rationality, I sometimes wonder if my mountainside epiphany is just my imagination. And I'm confronted with one of the hardest parts of my job as a spiritual-travel-writer: all of the most important things can't be described in words. This is akin to writing about art without ever being able to show anyone a painting. You can find approximations, but there's still a huge gap between the reality and your words.

One of the ways mystics try to get around this is the *via negativa*, which is Latin for the "negative way." Because the holy can never be captured in human concepts or words, the closest we can come to defining it is to say what it is not. Or simply to be quiet. As the prophet Elijah puts it, God is not in the whirlwind, God is not in the earthquake, God is not in the fire. God is in the still, small voice. The mystics are fond of this approach because they keep having experiences that can't be explained. In the end, what they learn comes down to a deep, unshakeable sense of truth. I can't convince you of mine, no more than you can convince me of yours.

But I can do this: I can tell you to visit Bear Butte, or another holy place that calls to you. I can advise you to sit on the side of a mountain and pray, but not try too hard, because simply gazing up at the clouds and feeling the wind on your face is often prayer enough. Sometimes revelations come. You might discover that you're an eagle or a spider, or you may hear God speaking to you through a burning bush, as Moses did when he went into the wilderness. Probably you'll just come back down the mountain a little clearer and calmer. And who's to say that's not a miracle in its own right?

When my skeptical side emerges (it's not fully developed, but it occasionally makes an appearance), I counter my doubts by thinking of all the times I've sat on the side of Bear Butte. I marvel at the number of helpers along the spiritual path, both human and non-human, ready to assist us if we just remain open to them. For me, one of these is the bear: strong, fierce, and wild.

❧

The spring after my insight on Bear Butte, I went to Peru, the same trip during which Rich's memory was a constant companion. After visiting Machu Picchu, our group flew to a remote lodge in the rainforest. One day I went on a hike through the jungle with a group of other writers. It was a long, hard slog of a walk, most of it through ankle-deep mud. My companion for much of the hike was a woman I didn't know very well, a writer who also produces documentary films.

After several hours of difficult trekking, we'd pretty much exhausted all trivial subjects, and the subject turned to spirit animals. I told her that I'd recently discovered I was a bear, slipping into the kind of easy candor that airplane passengers sometimes experience when sitting next to each other on long flights.

Instead of thinking I was crazy, Brandy was intrigued.

"I've always wondered if I had a spirit animal," she said. "How can I find out?"

I stopped and looked at her. She had also paused and was leaning on her walking stick as she pushed the hair back from her sweat-drenched face. Like me, she was spattered with mud, disheveled, and weary. In normal circumstances, I probably wouldn't have been so blunt, but the words came out of my mouth of their own volition.

"You're a bear," I said, realizing at some deep level that we shared this kinship, even though I barely knew her.

She looked at me in astonishment. "I've always been drawn to bears," she said. "And last week I got funding for my next film project, which is about bears."

We recognize each other, we bears, whether we're in the Black Hills of South Dakota or the rainforests of Peru. I spent much of the rest of our hike telling her why she needed to visit Bear Butte.

Kumbum Chamtse Ling Temple in Bloomington, Indiana

CHAPTER 11

NOT ALWAYS SO

I can, with one eye squinted, take it all as a blessing.
Flannery O'Connor

~ PILGRIMAGE ~
Kumbum Chamtse Ling Temple in Bloomington, Indiana

If you've watched enough nature documentaries, the following scene will likely be familiar to you.

A bear grazes in the vegetation bordering a rushing stream in the wilderness, contentedly munching berries as she lumbers along. Peaceful music plays, the sun is shining, and birds are twittering. Then the bear perceives a threat and the mood abruptly shifts. The music darkens as the huge, shaggy beast rises up on her hind legs, opens her mouth to expose her sharp teeth, and roars.

I am that bear. I am yelling at my priest. And we are standing at the altar at All Saints.

The journey that got me to this point had started without my even being aware of it. Because of its location in a university town, All Saints'

189

membership was more fluid than many faith communities, with people coming and going each year due to job changes or the completion of academic degrees. A number of people I'd grown close to had either died or moved away. All Saints felt different from the place we'd joined 20 years earlier, or even a decade ago when I'd been ordained.

Mel, an enthusiastic supporter of our Healing Touch ministry, had reached retirement age, and a new rector had been hired. Under her leadership the changes accelerated, a process that I watched with growing concern.

One reason for my disaffection was that the theological pendulum at All Saints had swung from the experiential to the intellectual. This was always a possibility in a church with so many academics, but before there were enough of us who valued a more emotionally engaging form of spirituality to provide balance. The current atmosphere reminded me of a line from the writer Nancy Mairs, who described the Protestantism of her childhood as having had "all the mystery scrubbed out of it by a vigorous and slightly vinegary reason."

At All Saints, the changes included an increased emphasis on the proper way of doing the liturgy. Those of us who served at the altar had to follow strict rules on minutiae such as the proper way to bow and exactly where to stand.

I knew that beautifully choreographed liturgies are an Anglican specialty. Think of the graceful and stately services in English cathedrals, connecting worshippers with centuries of tradition and engaging all their senses in beauty. But at All Saints, too often the liturgy reminded me of a church service I once attended in Istanbul. At first I was entranced by the grandeur of the Greek Orthodox pageantry, with its priests and altar servers dressed in elaborate vestments, surrounded by clouds of incense. But in the midst of my reverie, an usher appeared out of nowhere to rap me sharply on my knee with a cane. He motioned for me to uncross my legs—apparently the rules said my feet had to be flat on the floor. The rest of the service was a tedious blur, because once the spirit flees, it's hard to coax it back.

All Saints changed in other ways as well, taking on a more corpo rate organizational style, with decisions made by just a few people and information tightly controlled. I tried to express my concerns that the church was going in the wrong direction. I listened, watched, pondered, prayed, and felt increasingly helpless. Then I tried simply ignoring the difficulties, but that approach didn't work either.

It felt as if a wall was being built between an inner circle and the rest of the church. And I found, to my dismay, that I was on the outside. This was a shock, for I'd been on the inside so long that I'd forgotten what it was like to be on the other side of the gate, looking in.

One day I returned to the church on a quiet weekday afternoon after a three-week absence. When I entered I saw that the front room was set with tables and chairs. There was obviously going to be a dinner of some sort that evening. The priest was wandering among the tables, adjusting the placement of the glasses, making sure the napkins were folded correctly, lining up the silverware. She looked up at me briefly, acknowledging my presence with a disinterested nod.

It felt like the enactment of a parable, for in the Gospels Jesus often uses the metaphor of a banquet to describe the Kingdom of Heaven. Only I was not among those invited to the feast.

The Dreary Side of Church

I knew that leadership transitions are often difficult for parishes, as I'd weathered them before. Over the years I'd been part of conversations with dissatisfied parishioners debating whether to leave, both at All Saints and in other faith communities. For whatever reason, they'd gotten their feelings hurt. They didn't like a political stance the denomination had taken. They disapproved of the way the church was spending its budget. Again and again I'd said some variation of this: "The church isn't perfect. It makes mistakes. But it's a family, and you don't leave a family just because Aunt Edna drives you crazy every Thanksgiving. You stick it out because that's what it means to be in community. Clergy and other leaders come and go, but the church remains."

I still believe this. I think that most of the time, people should stay, especially if it's a community in which they've invested years. Too often parishioners leave over difficulties that will eventually resolve themselves. Being part of a church is not primarily about making you feel happy, which is a temporary state not directly connected to spiritual growth. If you're feeling chipper and content on Sunday mornings, it's a bonus, not a requirement.

But when I was the one whose unhappiness was growing, all of these arguments weren't as convincing. It felt as if All Saints was losing its way, and in the process I was losing mine as well, becoming a person I didn't want to be: judgmental, angry, resentful.

As each Sunday passed at All Saints, more and more of what had once been meaningful to me dribbled away. I still cared for my fellow parishioners, and I enjoyed visiting with them before and after the services. But the rituals had become hollow. Years before I'd come to see the limitations of spirituality without the supporting structure of a religion; now I was experiencing its mirror image.

One Sunday morning, I realized that I hadn't actually worshipped there in more than a year. I'd knelt for the prayers, crossed myself at all the appropriate times, sang the hymns, and took communion. But none of these actions had been more than superficial and rote.

❦

As I began to take seriously the possibility of leaving All Saints, a great sadness came over me, one that dogged my heels every time I entered the church and kept me awake at night for long, restless hours. After more than 20 years, I still remembered how hard it had been leaving the Unitarian Universalists; the prospect of leaving All Saints was far more painful. This church was where we'd baptized our sons and mourned the death of friends. I'd preached from its pulpit, comforted its parishioners, taught its education classes, and mowed its grass. In the room overlooking its courtyard I'd been part of hundreds of Healing Touch sessions. I'd stood at its altar and made vows to serve the Church, both with a big "C" and a little "c." There was that private vow I'd made, too, the one where I pledged to remain at All Saints for the rest of my life.

On Sundays, I looked at people as they came to the altar for communion. Seeing them receive the bread and wine, their faces open and vulnerable, was one of the things I loved about serving at the altar. I knew many of their private hurts—whose child was struggling in school, whose brother was an alcoholic, who was waiting for the results of a biopsy. Now each face made me realize what I was losing.

Bob was less enmeshed in the church than I was, but he had his own ties and memories. He'd been involved in many ministries through the years, from adult education to being on the buildings and grounds committee in seeming perpetuity. There was hardly a square inch of All Saints that he hadn't painted, patched, repaired, or renovated.

But the experience of being at All Saints put us in such a low mood that it took days to recover. Every Sunday felt like a funeral—not the celebration that comes at the end of a long and well-lived life, but the kind where you mourn all the possibilities that have been cut short.

"This isn't how church is supposed to be," I said as we returned home from All Saints one Sunday.

"Well, the martyrs didn't have a very good time in church either," Bob said. "At least there's no burning of heretics."

During this time, I came to understand as never before the ways in which churches draw boundaries. Historically, the lines between us-and-them have often been based on race, social class, politics, sexual orientation, or even something as trivial as what type of music you like. The message is given, sometimes in subtle and sometimes in obvious ways, that the community is open only to certain types of people. The banquet table has reserved seats.

And when that happens, I've come to believe that sometimes people *do* need to leave, especially if remaining in that place confines them to a spiritual desert. I don't think God wants us to remain in that desert forever. Look it up in the Bible—Moses led his people out of one. It took 40 years, but eventually they got out. And the New Testament does not have a single verse that says you have to stay in a church that's making you miserable.

❧

Which brings me back to the scene at the altar during which I yelled at my priest. It wasn't during a service, thankfully—I had a bit more discretion than that. About the only thing I can say in my defense is that it was three days after Rich's death and I was exhausted and grieving.

The trigger for our argument was small. As I was talking to the music director about hymns for Rich's upcoming funeral, our priest interrupted our conversation. I couldn't talk to him on my own, she said, because all discussions of the funeral had to take place in her presence. She would hold a meeting on Monday to discuss details.

I looked at her and realized she had no idea what I'd just been through. After a year at All Saints, she didn't know either Rich or me. In one sense it wasn't her fault, as the message she'd somehow received—whether in seminary or in former church jobs or from the All Saints vestry—is that the job of a priest is to be an administrator, not a good shepherd, and that compassion is a task that can be delegated to other people in the parish.

I'd never raised my voice in anger to another adult. I was a deacon and a Girl Citizen who'd been raised in quite possibly the nicest small town in the entire Midwest. But I expressed my opinion quite forcefully, and then for good measure I added my general estimation of how things were going at All Saints.

My behavior was rude and unprofessional. But here's a curious thing: it seemed like I was channeling something more than my ordinary self. And that something was connected to my epiphany on Bear Butte and to the dozens of pilgrimages I'd made there over the years. I felt as if I was ten feet tall and could tear out a tree by its roots with my paws. My identity had indeed shifted, there on the side of the mountain. Whether it was becoming a bear, or declining estrogen levels, or just not caring as much as I once had about what others thought of me, I was different than I'd been before.

The priest—who hadn't expected to need bear spray in church that morning—looked both shocked and a little scared.

"A church is no place for an argument," she said, and then turned on her heel to walk away from me.

She was wrong: many of history's most important arguments have taken place in churches, a fact I knew from following in Martin Luther's steps in Wittenberg. On my way out of All Saints that morning, I could have pounded my own 95 Theses on the front door.

The Buddha Knocks on the Sacristy Door

I think there's good evidence that God has both a sense of humor (example: camels) as well as a finely developed sense of irony. In my own life, the evidence for this is that my last year at All Saints became a boot camp in Buddhism.

I'd dabbled in Buddhism in my 20s, and in my travels I'd been to many Buddhist temples and shrines whose beauty and serenity greatly attracted me. My inability to meditate, however, kept me from exploring this faith in any depth, and eventually I moved on to other spiritual paths.

But my troubles at All Saints made me turn to Buddhism again, not because I had much hope that its teachings would be helpful, but because Christianity felt like such a dead end. The practices that had been meaningful to me in the past—prayer, communion, Healing Touch—did little to ease the ache in my heart or give me guidance on how to move forward.

Once again, I turned to books for guidance. Some were Buddhist texts I'd read before and not found particularly engaging, but now pages often spoke directly to me. It's amazing how this works: the words are exactly the same, yet we hear them differently depending upon where we are in our lives. Explain to me how this can happen unless books have spiritual power.

I came to appreciate as never before Buddhism's psychological insights and its practical approach to the universal dilemmas of human experience. Buddhism, more than any other religion, has spent millennia studying the workings of the mind and the harmful illusions it creates. The First Noble Truth taught by the Buddha is that life is suffering, and the Second Noble Truth is that desire and ignorance keep us trapped in suffering. The only way out of this cycle of despair is to train our minds to see beyond the tricks it plays on us.

During this time, it helped me to view All Saints as a training ground in Buddhist practice, a place that was forcing me to confront realities about myself and the nature of existence. I saw the ways in which ego played a role in my dissatisfaction at All Saints. While the parish had problems, I couldn't deny that I was also hosting an extended and elaborate pity party for myself. I'd enjoyed being on the inside all those years; being on the outside was like sandpaper to my ego. I also recognized that a Buddhist teacher would say this was good for my spiritual development.

"This is why there aren't more Buddhists in the world," I snapped at the imaginary sage who insisted upon giving me unsolicited advice. "Nobody but a masochist would willingly sign up for this process."

The Buddhist teachings on impermanence gave me greater comfort. Years before a Japanese monk said this when I asked him the central truth of Buddhism: "Not always so."

At the time it struck me as a pretty meager philosophy, even though he'd used three times as many words as had the Trappist monk at Gethsemani. Now I recognized it as one of the most profound pieces of wisdom I'd ever received. Not always so. Everything changes; everything is temporary. My sorrow at All Saints sprang in part from trying to make it what it had once been. The parish of the past was different from what it was now, and I couldn't keep mourning what was gone.

I also appreciated how Buddhists don't try as hard as Christians to make you love everybody. Oh, this commandment sounds good in theory, and Jesus and the saints followed it successfully. But sometimes the Christian admonition to love is simply too much. In my unhappiness at All Saints, most of the time the best I could manage in church was a dignified detachment—except, of course, for the bear attack at the altar, which had significantly reinforced my position as an outsider.

Love and mindfulness—the ability to live fully in the present moment—are part of both Christianity and Buddhism. The problem is that in both traditions, believers are very good at turning these tenets to their own selfish advantage. Buddhist precepts on mindfulness can become an excuse for narcissism, while Christian teachings on love and forgiveness can be used to manipulate people, which is one of the reasons why churches have such a hard time dealing with conflict.

My most valued companion during this time was Pema Chödrön, a Tibetan Buddhist nun who wrote the definitive guide on what to do when the shit hits the fan. *When Things Fall Apart: Heart Advice for Difficult Times* was one of those books I'd tried reading before that hadn't held my attention. Now every page had some kernel of wisdom that I pondered for days.

Chödrön writes of the lessons to be found in disintegration, failure, and sadness. Quoting her teacher Chögyam Trungpa Rinpoche, she says, "Chaos should be regarded as extremely good news." That's because this state can shake us out of our complacency and leave us raw and exposed, stripping away the pretense that we're in control and shocking us into an awareness of the present moment.

Instead of panicking or falling into despair, Chödrön says we can approach the turmoil with curiosity, asking what it can teach us. We should resist the urge to immediately find solace or distraction in something else. Sitting with the disappointment, fear, and frustration humbles us and helps us see the games we play to bolster our ego. This process can awaken us to our true natures—the word Buddhism, in fact, comes from the Sanskrit *budhi*, which simply means to "wake up."

"When everything falls apart and we feel uncertainty, disappointment, shock, embarrassment, what's left is a mind that is clear, unbiased, and fresh," Chödrön writes.

And once we're in that state, new possibilities emerge. Here was the line in Chödrön's book that spoke to me the most: "Everything that ends is also the beginning of something else."

It was pretty clear what was dying for me, but what was being born?

To Tibet by Way of Indiana

An old adage says that when the student is ready, the teacher will appear. In my case, he appeared in the little-known spiritual mecca of Bloomington, Indiana, and he was accompanied by a tufted titmouse.

I'd been to Bloomington several years before to write about its Kumbum Chamtse Ling Temple, which is one of the most important centers for Tibetan Buddhism in North America. During my visit I became fascinated by this thriving oasis of Tibetan and Mongolian culture in the Midwest, which reinforced for me the fact that holy sites can pop up in the most unexpected places.

The temple was established by Thubten Jigme Norbu, the eldest brother of the Fourteenth Dalai Lama. Norbu escaped Tibet in 1950 and was one of the first Tibetans to be granted political asylum in the United States. After coming to Indiana University in Bloomington, he established its program in Tibetan Studies. Throughout his life he was a passionate advocate for his nation, helping to publicize human rights abuses in Tibet, campaigning for Tibetan independence, and educating students about his native culture and its religious traditions. In 1979 he founded the Tibetan Mongolian Buddhist Cultural Center, which is affiliated with the temple.

This Indiana holy site is part of an ancient tradition. Buddhism spread from India to the Himalayas during the eighth through tenth centuries. In Tibet, it mingled with indigenous, shamanistic religious practices, producing a faith that's quite distinct from other forms of

Buddhism. Tibetan Buddhism places particular emphasis on the idea of *bodhisattvas*, those who've pledged to forego final liberation until all sentient beings are enlightened. It also believes that its greatest teachers, known as lamas, have the ability to return over multiple lifetimes. The Dalai Lama is held in highest reverence in Tibetan Buddhism, but other reincarnated lamas are also honored as enlightened teachers.

In Bloomington, a colorfully decorated, Tibetan-style gate marks the entrance to the Buddhist complex, which includes nearly a dozen buildings on 108 wooded acres in a suburban corner of the city. Inside the gate, the first structure is the cultural center, which has information on the history of the Kumbum Chamtse Ling Temple. There I learned that Chamtse Ling means "field of compassion" in Tibetan, while Kumbum is the name of one of the most important monasteries in Tibet. The Fourteenth Dalai Lama granted this name because he sees the Bloomington temple as the western counterpart of the Tibetan Kumbum. He himself maintains such close ties to the community that he has his own apartment there.

As I ventured farther into the complex, I passed two stupas, structures that are used as a focus for walking meditation. The first, the Jangchub Chorten, was dedicated by the Dalai Lama in 1987 to honor Tibetan refugees. He returned to Bloomington in 1999 to establish the second shrine, the Kalachakra Stupa, as a place to pray for world peace.

Between the stupas is the Mani Korlo, a structure containing large Tibetan prayer wheels. The three-foot bronze wheels come from Tibet's Kumbum Monastery and are filled with more than 800,000,000 copies of the *Om Mani Padme Hum* mantra, a central prayer in Buddhism. It's believed that when a person turns one of these wheels, blessings will be bestowed upon all beings.

As I moved a wheel on its spindle, I thought of the Tibetan prayer flags hanging in my home garden, their more ephemeral counterpart. I liked the idea that even on a day when I can't muster up a single amen, these spiritual tools could help me, their prayers released by each gust of wind:

As Wind carries our prayers for Earth and All Life,
May respect and love light our way.
May our hearts be filled with compassion for others and for ourselves.
May peace increase on Earth.
May it begin with me.

At last I came to the heart of this holy site: the Kumbum Chamtse Ling Temple, a two-story, rectangular building with red columns at its entrance and a roof topped by a golden Dharma wheel, its eight spokes representing the central tenets of Buddhist belief. After I entered and took off my shoes, a guide brought me to its shrine room. She pointed out the Sanskrit sign above its door.

"It says that all who enter this room should have a pure heart, so please lay your negative thoughts and worries outside this door," she said. "Don't worry—you can pick them up again on the way out."

Inside, I admired the Tibetan Buddhist iconography that filled the room, including paintings of Buddhas and *bodhisattvas* in bold colors on the walls and gilded statues on its altar. I was surprised to also see sacred objects from other faiths, from a Quran and Jewish shofar to a *Book of Common Prayer.* My guide explained that members of eleven spiritual traditions were present when the Dalai Lama consecrated the temple in 2003, and that people of all faiths continue to be welcome.

During the prayer service, I marveled at the resiliency of this tradition that's found fertile ground so far from its homeland high in the Himalayas. When the robed monk at the altar began to chant, I sensed that the holy was as present here as in the suburban churches just down the street, outside the gate that marks where Indiana ends and Tibet begins.

❧

It was a serendipitous invitation that brought me back to the Kumbum Chamtse Ling Temple during my existential crisis at All Saints. A friend who was a member of its community heard that Bob and I were going to be in the area and arranged for us to have a private audience with the Venerable Arjia Rinpoche, the spiritual leader of the center.

When I'd been at the temple before, I'd not had the chance to meet Rinpoche, as he's affectionately known in the community (the term, pronounced rin-poe-che, means "precious one" in Tibetan and is a title given to an esteemed teacher who's believed to be a reincarnated sage). But I knew his story from his autobiography, *Surviving the Dragon: A Tibetan Lama's Account of 40 Years Under Chinese Rule.*

Of Mongolian descent, Rinpoche was recognized at the age of two as the reincarnated abbot of Kumbum Monastery. He spent his early childhood being trained as a spiritual leader, until the Chinese government took over his monastery. Many of its members were tortured and Rinpoche was sent to a labor camp for 16 years. Eventually his usefulness was recognized by the authorities, who appointed him as abbot of his former monastery, only this time under their control. In 1998 he could no longer in good conscience continue to serve as its leader and escaped to the U.S. As one of the highest-ranking Tibetan lamas to have fled to the West, he was appointed by the Dalai Lama in 2005 to serve as the director of the center in Bloomington.

Rinpoche's dramatic life story passed through my mind as Bob and I entered his modest home on the grounds of the temple complex. On the outside it looked like a standard ranch-style house; inside we traveled 7,000 miles to Tibet. The smell of incense lingered in the air and its walls were covered with brightly colored Tibetan paintings.

After removing our shoes, we were ushered into a small sitting room by a young monk in a maroon robe, who served us tea and a multi-layered, homemade cake. As I sipped the tea, I grew a bit nervous, for while I was eager to meet Rinpoche, I'd no idea what we'd find to talk about for very long.

A few minutes later he appeared, and I soon realized that my apprehension was unwarranted. I was struck by how similar his serene manner was to that of the Dalai Lama, whom I'd seen the year before on one of his American visits. But instead of being on a stage in front of thousands of people, this man was sitting in a chair next to us, beaming with welcome, urging us to have another cup of tea and more cake. Despite a schedule that was undoubtedly filled with far more important things than greeting two strangers from Iowa, he acted as if we were members of his family who'd returned after an extended time away.

We visited for nearly an hour with Rinpoche, speaking first about the center in Bloomington and then about the challenges faced by the Tibetan Buddhist community in exile. He told us about a hospital he'd helped establish in Mongolia to treat children with cancer. The only time a shadow passed over his features was when he told us that he wasn't allowed to return to his home in Tibet, even to visit.

Then, because we felt so comfortable, the conversation turned more personal. To my surprise, I found myself telling him about my troubles at All Saints. He listened intently to my story, nodding throughout. At the end, I asked if similar situations ever happened in Buddhism.

"Oh, yes," he said, in his accented but excellent English. "This is not uncommon."

"What should I do?" I asked.

"In every bad situation, there is an exchange that can happen," he said. "Every bad thing has a possible good thing that can come from it. You need to search for that good thing."

In one sense his advice wasn't especially profound—for honestly, most spiritual truths aren't that complicated, at least until you try to put them into practice. But as he spoke those words, I thought of his own life story, one filled with tragedy and loss. My own difficulties seemed remarkably small next to what he'd endured, and yet he was responding to my story with patient attention. Often the greatest spiritual gift we can receive is someone who really listens to us.

Our guide had told us that when Rinpoche visits Mongolia, people line the streets and hold up their babies, because simply having him look upon them is said to confer a blessing. Sitting across from him in that cozy room, this practice wasn't at all surprising to me. The kindness and compassion in his gaze warmed my bruised heart as much as his words.

And then Bob interrupted us.

"Oh, look!" he said, pointing to a bird perched on the railing of the deck just outside the window. "It's a tufted titmouse. She's carrying grass for the nest she's building."

I shot a glance at Bob, the sort of look a wife gives her husband when he interrupts her conversation with a Tibetan lama by pointing out a tufted titmouse. But when Rinpoche turned around to see the bird, a smile spread over his face.

"Oh, how wonderful!" he exclaimed.

For several minutes we all admired the little bird that was warming herself in the spring sunshine. Then she flew off to return to her task of nest building and we continued our talk, the conversation shifting to other topics.

It was only later that I realized the significance of Rinpoche's reaction to the bird. I'd read thousands of words that tried to convey what it means to live in the present moment, but until being in Rinpoche's presence their truth hadn't penetrated. Rinpoche was fully *there* with us. We were strangers to him, and yet he delighted in us. The bird also came as a stranger to him, and he delighted equally in her arrival. For the entire time she was with us, his attention was totally on her. This is what can happen, I realized, when you devote your life to Buddhist practice.

And I recognized this as well: that Rinpoche was filled with more *agape*, the selfless love celebrated in the Bible, than any Christian I'd met in a long time.

At the end of our time together, Rinpoche presented us with *khatas*, the Buddhist scarves that I recognized from Thomas Merton's grave at the Abbey of Gethsemani. He put them over our heads and then took both of our hands in his as he thanked us for coming.

"Would you be willing to give us a blessing before we go?" I asked.

"Of course," he said.

I'd expected a brief prayer, but instead Rinpoche directed us to sit down again and chanted over us for perhaps ten minutes in Tibetan, his voice rising and falling in unfamiliar syllables that enfolded us in grace. We didn't need to understand the words to know that we were being given a precious gift.

Sitting there, I felt welcomed, appreciated, and loved—and at the same time, even sadder in the knowledge that my path was leading me away from All Saints.

❦

On our last Sunday at All Saints, only a handful of people knew we were leaving. That afternoon I was to meet with my bishop to get formal approval for a sabbatical from All Saints, a leave that I intended to make permanent. Throughout the service I tried to distract myself and not think that this was my final Sunday at a church where I'd spent more than two decades. Afterwards I greeted and hugged people, took off my robe for the last time, and met Bob in the back hallway.

"Time to leave," I said.

"Let's stop in the healing room and pick up the plants," Bob said. "No one's going to water them when we're gone."

We walked out the back door, carrying the plants in our hands. I wasn't surprised to see that they were already dead.

Iona, Scotland

CHAPTER 12

THE CHURCH OF GOD'S ODDS AND ENDS

Come, come, whoever you are.
Wanderer, worshipper, lover of leaving—it doesn't matter,
Ours is not a caravan of despair.
Come, even if you have broken your vow a hundred times,
Come, come again, come.

Rumi

~ PILGRIMAGE ~
Iona in Scotland

In the year 563, a middle-aged monk was forced to leave his native Ireland because of bad behavior. While the story is a little muddled, it involved a copy of a psalter—a book of psalms—that Columba had made without permission from its owner. Things got a little out of hand, as they sometimes do in church politics, and then they got a lot out of hand, and then there was a battle in which thousands of men were killed.

A synod of church leaders found Columba responsible. At first they were going to excommunicate him, but then an alternative was proposed: he could instead go into exile, leaving Ireland and not stopping until he came to a place where he could no longer see his homeland. Columba set out by boat and ended up on the island of Iona, a tiny slip of land off the western coast of Scotland. Upon reaching it, he stood on its highest point and looked back to see if Ireland was still in view. When he couldn't glimpse its shore, he knew that he'd fulfilled his penance and found his new home.

And if you go to Iona today, you can stand upon a hill that's known in Gaelic as *Carn Cuil ri Eirinn*, "the cairn with its back to Ireland." Even after fourteen centuries, the land remembers.

∽

Columba traveled by boat across the sea to Iona. Back in Iowa, Bob and I drove five miles by car to the neighboring town of Coralville—and of all the journeys described in this book, this was the longest.

We landed in a much smaller Episcopal parish, one that met in a building that reminded me more of a 1970s ranch house than a church. The first Sunday I sat and sniffled through most of the service. Though I'd asked for approval from the bishop to spend my sabbatical there, I still felt like a lost sheep that had wandered into the wrong pasture.

So much was missing in this church. I'd always loved holy places filled with color and ornamentation, and this sanctuary had very little of it. There were no pews, no kneelers, no organ, and just a little stained glass. The elevator was unusual, too, a strange contraption that carried people on an open platform between the main floor of the church and the basement, making them look like performers in a magic act as they appeared and disappeared. This added to the somewhat surreal experience of being in a new place on a Sunday morning, sitting among people largely unknown to me.

Episcopal liturgies being much the same between churches, the service had a familiar feel. But afterwards, the announcements were different from what I expected. Instead of people talking about upcoming meetings or tasks that needed volunteers, they shared what they were thankful for that week, from the birth of a grandchild to a new apartment they'd been able to move into because of the generosity of church members. Someone asked for prayers for a friend whose daughter had died, and another spoke about the failing health of her parents. I was struck by the vulnerability they displayed.

When we came back the next Sunday, it felt a little less foreign. The music, especially, drew us in, both because of the choice of songs and the way the sound reverberated in that small space. Someone sitting in the back had a baritone voice so strong I could feel my chair vibrating.

At the social hour after the service, a parishioner welcomed me and then said, "Once you get to know us, you'll realize this church is full of God's odds and ends."

Over the next weeks, I began to see the ways in which this was true. Many members of the parish had experienced tough times in their personal lives; others had been burned by established religion and were still wary of it. The church's hierarchical structure was blurred because it had no paid clergy; instead, four priests volunteered their time. Without a big budget, people pitched in and did everything from scrubbing toilets to giving sermons, saving money so that the parish could give a substantial amount to charity each year. Outside of church, many volunteered at places that served those pushed to the edges of society, from the local food pantry to a crisis center.

On the Sunday when the church commissioned new volunteers for the year, people weren't invited to the altar, because almost everyone was getting sworn in and there wasn't room for them up front. So people just stood up where they were and the priest serving that morning blessed them en masse.

Bob took to the parish immediately. "I'm really not that much of a high church sort of guy," he said. "I like the laid-back feel of this place."

Within a month, he was helping out with adult education and pitching in on painting projects. If Bob ever gets portrayed in a stained glass window (unlikely, I realize, but you never know), he's going to have a paintbrush in his hand: St. Bob, patron of philosophical handymen.

I was more hesitant about joining in. During my sabbatical, I was happy to take a break from ecclesiastical duties, having experienced firsthand the old saying that the closer you are to the altar, the farther you are from God. On Sunday mornings, I appreciated the fact that all I had to do was show up. And some Sundays, I didn't do even that.

I clung to something once said by Flannery O'Connor, that wise chronicler of belief, doubt, and weirdness: "Faith comes and goes. It rises and falls like the tides of an invisible ocean. If it is presumptuous to think that faith will stay with you forever, it is just as presumptuous to think that unbelief will."

The Outcast Becomes a Saint

Meanwhile, Columba was settling into life on Iona. He actually wasn't alone, because he brought with him a dozen disciples, men who'd helped him establish several monasteries in Ireland. On Iona, they started building another new monastery. Columba vowed to convert as many unbelievers to Christ as had been killed in the battle he caused.

One of many amazing things about Columba is that he fulfilled his vow—and then some. While much of Europe was still mired in the chaos left after the collapse of the Roman Empire, his monastery on Iona became a school for missionaries who brought Christianity to places throughout the British Isles. Despite Iona's remote location and small size—just a little more than three miles long and a mile wide—the island became one of the most important centers for Christianity in Europe.

Columba's long-standing passion for books made Iona an educational center as well as a religious one. During a period when manuscripts were rare and precious, he and his followers copied hundreds of volumes, helping to keep literacy alive when it was fading in other parts of Europe. He wrote poems and songs and also became active in the politics of Scotland, serving as an advisor to its warrior kings and fostering and educating their princely sons at Iona.

Columba was a man of diverse talents: he was said to be able to calm the sea with his prayers, prophesy the future, and heal the sick. In addition, two firsts are credited to him. He's believed to have launched the first copyright dispute in history, a battle over who owned the manuscript he'd copied from another text. He lost the case, but he still gets credit for raising the issue. And he was the first person to encounter the Loch Ness Monster, described as a huge water beast that Columba banished to the bottom of the River Ness.

There's another story that I love about Columba. After he became well-known as a man of learning and holiness in his new home, the Irish invited him back to settle a dispute involving clergy, nobles, and the pagan bards who were still hanging around, even though much of the island had converted to Christianity. Columba accepted, but because of the earlier judgment that had been rendered against him, he traveled blindfolded and with the sod of Iona tied to the bottom of his sandals. He was able to keep to the letter of his punishment even as he brokered peace between the various parties.

I might be mistaken, but this story makes me wonder if Columba didn't have a sly sense of humor. Surely those who invited him back to Ireland didn't expect him to go to such elaborate measures. I can hear him saying to them, "Sorry that I'm leaving clods of dirt all over. And don't mind this blindfold—I'm wearing it so I won't see the place that kicked me out."

By the time Columba died at the age of 76, he was already regarded as a saint. As an indication of his fame, in subsequent centuries Iona's graveyard became the final resting place for kings from Ireland, Scotland, and Norway, all of whom wanted to spend eternity next to him. And in a final piece of irony, Ireland now claims him (along with St. Patrick and St. Brigit) as one of its three patron saints. As far as I know, no Irish statues depict him wearing a blindfold.

After Columba's death, the monastic settlement on Iona continued to grow, at its height having 150 monks in residence. Satellite monasteries and churches in Scotland, Ireland, and Northumbria in England looked to it for guidance. Its treasures included four intricately carved, twenty-foot stone crosses (even after the Celts converted to Christianity, they still used stones to mark holy ground). The stones bore the Celtic cross, which has a circle where the vertical and horizontal bars come together—a symbolic blending of the new faith with an older tradition that loved to use circles and spirals in its own sacred art.

The literary traditions established by Columba came to full flower in the eighth century, when scribes at the Iona monastery began work on what's been called the most beautiful book in the world: the *Book of Kells*, a Latin manuscript of the Gospels. Made from the finest vellum and painted with inks and pigments from around the world, its words are surrounded by a menagerie of figures and creatures—Christ and the saints, mythical animals like dragons and sea serpents, and playful cats, darting dogs, and mice fighting over pieces of communion bread.

The sensuous colors leap off the pages, brilliant blues, reds, golds, and greens interwoven in complex knots and swirling ribbons.

All of this artistic, cultural, and religious vitality came to an end, alas, as a result of my ancestors. The Vikings first came calling around 800 and destroyed the monastic community on the island during a series of raids, killing its monks and stealing its church treasures. The *Book of Kells*, thankfully, was spirited away before the Vikings found it.

Iona settled back into slumber, its beaches scoured by the wild Atlantic surf, its grassy hills and sand dunes buffeted by winter winds and warmed by summer sunshine.

Setting Out in a Little Boat on the Sea

Bob and I and our sons visited Iona during the semester we lived in England. First we drove forever across Scotland, then we took a ferry to the island of Mull, where we drove another long and winding road, and then we boarded yet another ferry to get to Iona. With two young boys in the car, it felt at times like a penitential pilgrimage.

Once we arrived on the island, I was surprised that such a small place could have such a large influence on the world, both in the past and today—because Iona is once again a center for spirituality.

The current revival began in 1938, when Church of Scotland minister George MacLeod founded the Iona Community on the island. Under his leadership, the ecumenical group spearheaded the restoration of a Benedictine monastery that had been constructed there around 1200. Today community members lead worship services and retreat programs for the thousands of pilgrims who come to Iona each year. Iona prayers, hymns, and liturgies have been widely reprinted and have played a significant role in the revival of interest in Celtic Christian spirituality.

While the physical landscape of Iona is dominated by the abbey built well after Columba's time, its spiritual landscape is infused with memories of Columba and the earliest Christian residents of the island. Nearly every square foot of Iona has a story associated with it, some legendary and some based in fact.

We followed the standard tourist routine on Iona, touring the abbey and the nearby ruins of a twelfth-century nunnery, strolling through its cemetery, and walking the shoreline. It was a bright, sunny day, unusual for Scotland, with a breeze that was invigorating rather than blustery, as the winds of the Inner Hebrides can often be. As we explored the island, I recalled that Iona may have been a holy place for the Druids before the Christians arrived. It felt to me like a place that's been steeped in prayers for many centuries.

Looking back, my memories of the island blend with other holy places we visited during the months we lived in Yorkshire. On our travels we explored sacred sites both small and large: holy wells and roadside shrines adorned with homemade crosses, and prehistoric landmarks such as Newgrange, a Neolithic passage tomb north of Dublin, a thousand years older than Stonehenge. We hiked across farm fields in search of stone circles and walked through ruined abbeys and monasteries shrouded in misty rain, their broken-down walls overgrown with moss.

Through visiting these sites and learning about Celtic Christian history, I came to understand pilgrimage in a new way. Like many, I'd thought of pilgrimage as a journey, a visit to a place like Lourdes or Rome, followed by a return to ordinary life. The Celts, in contrast, viewed pilgrimage as the guiding principle of their entire lives. We are always on a pilgrim's journey, they believed. We are all *hospites mundi*, guests of the world.

I suspect this philosophy evolved in part because of a perennial sense of wanderlust in Celtic culture: pilgrimage has always provided a good excuse to get out of the house. Their legends and histories are full of journeys, from the sixth-century wanderings of St. Brendan the Navigator to the early twentieth-century Antarctic explorations of Ernest Shackleton.

On their travels, Celtic Christians sought out desolate and wild spots where the veil between worlds was thin, places that could help them be reborn in the spirit. In this they drew inspiration from Jesus, who often retreated to such places to pray, and from the third-century Desert Fathers and Mothers of Egypt. If you're looking for God, countless pilgrims have discovered it's best to go to a landscape with little to distract you.

Ireland being sorely lacking in deserts, pilgrims would also set out to find a "desert in the ocean," in the words of an early text. They'd launch themselves onto the sea in small coracles without oars or maps, trusting themselves entirely to God.

As we traveled during that semester, I became one of those wandering monks, seeking my place of resurrection, trusting that my steps would be guided. I was lonely at times, since Bob and the boys were often at school, and I missed my friends and ordinary routines. I don't think it was an accident that my call to ordination brewed during this period. The Celts knew that a major reason to go on pilgrimage is to uproot yourself from the comforts of home so that you have to depend upon God alone.

Ian Bradley, writing in his book *The Celtic Way,* tells the story of three monks who set out on one of those classic, foolish Irish pilgrimages. After a week of being tossed around by the sea, they finally washed up on the coast of Cornwall, where they were brought before King Alfred. When he asked them why they'd taken such a dangerous journey, they replied, "We stole away because we wanted for the love of God to be on pilgrimage, we cared not where."

Men after my own heart.

Finding God Here, There, and Everywhere

Some scholars get grumpy about the growing interest in Celtic Christianity, saying it's based as much on imagination as history (though imagination isn't necessarily a bad thing in religion, a fact that the Celts knew better than most). But there's certainly much we can learn from this tradition that flourished for centuries in a backwater corner of the Western world.

Many Christians today are drawn to this culture's deep love of the natural world. To the Celts, nature was a sacred book created by God, as worthy of study as the Bible. God was a close, constant presence, a belief likely influenced by the pre-Christian beliefs of the Celts, whose gods also lived close at hand in rivers, springs, and mountains. (Here's an interesting fact: unlike many Christians then and now, the newly converted Celts didn't have any trouble with the theological doctrine of the Trinity, because a number of their gods also came in sets of three.)

The Celts also bequeathed to their descendants an abiding faith in the power of words. They'd long consulted poets and storytellers for guidance and had great respect for how the spoken word could both heal and harm. After the coming of Christianity, this belief morphed into the custom of blessing. Celtic blessings weren't just sweet sentiments of affection, but rather actual conduits for divine grace. Think of this the next time you see a needlepointed Irish blessing—there's real power in the stitches.

The sense of the constant presence of God and the power of words were also found in the Celtic practice of interweaving even the most ordinary of actions with prayer. Nearly every part of life—washing dishes, getting ready for bed, greeting the rising sun—had prayers and invocations associated with it. Given how fond they were of journeying, it's no wonder that the Irish have so many blessings for travelers. "May the road rise up to meet you" is just one of many.

Even the most enthusiastic lovers of this tradition aren't so enamored with some of the other spiritual practices of the Celts. The early monks were great fans of penances designed to give them maximum discomfort, for example, including something known as the cross vigil, in which they would stand with hands outstretched as they prayed for hours. St. Kevin of Glendalough was said to do this for so long that birds would come and build nests in his palms.

These early Celtic Christians also had a strong sense for the power of evil, because they believed their world was populated by both positive and negative supernatural forces. Illness, famine, invasions from abroad, and tribal warfare at home meant that their lives were often harsh and short. God, the saints, and the angels were constantly being called upon for protection, often in breastplate or *lorica* prayers that could cast a circle of protection against evil. We who live comfortable, middle class lives tend to forget how most people have always lived, vulnerable to threats from without and within. The Celts knew far better than us the dangers that lurk in the world.

Given all of this, it's no wonder that a thread of melancholy runs through Celtic spirituality. You can sense it in their prayers and hear it in their music, which has undertones of sadness even in many of its liveliest tunes. In their wandering, in their praying, in their art, and in their music, the Celts have always known that light is shadowed with darkness.

I know that I could sense the shadows in those ruined abbeys slowly returning to earth, and on the lonely beaches of Iona, looking across the sea.

❧

Attending the Church of God's Odds and Ends during my sabbatical taught me something new about holy sites, a truth that I'd somehow missed in all my years of journeying. I knew already that the sacred is found in many types of places—in historic churches and golden shrines, amid prehistoric standing stones, on the sides of mountains and at the bedsides of the dying. But this church taught me that holy sites come and go.

Here's what I mean by this. If you visit this church on a weekday, it has all the spiritual oomph of a classroom. But if you come on a Sunday morning, if you sit and watch attentively as the space fills up with people, at a certain point it's as if the spirit swoops in, like it was just waiting for the rest of us to get there. This phenomenon is all the more dramatic and powerful because of the contrast.

I still love the magnificent sanctuaries of many faiths. With their glorious art and architecture, they're some of humanity's most creative endeavors. These places can give us glimpses of the glory of heaven while still on earth.

But I've come to believe that the future of religion, for American Christianity at least, may well lie in places like the Church of God's Odds and Ends—the scrappy little communities with small budgets and big hearts, who make do largely with volunteers. They're the Ionas of our post-modern world. On the edge of the map, away from the centers of ecclesiastical power, they're creating new models of worship and community in a world that's increasingly turning away from Christianity-as-usual.

When Columba sent his missionaries out to evangelize, he directed them to create "colonies of heaven" in the middle of their pagan neighbors. He knew that new converts would be drawn to these communities more by how their residents lived than by what they preached. Surely that's as true today as it was in Columba's time.

❧

After several months at the Church of God's Odds and Ends, some answers emerged. I realized that I'm still a Christian, though one who contains bits and pieces of the other faiths I've followed in my life (and given the fact I'm only in my mid-50s, I may still have another religion or two in my future). I know, too, that I'm unlikely to find a group of Lutheran-Wiccan-Unitarian-Bear-Buddhist-Episcopalians to hang out with, even if I move to a larger city. And in fact, I need a spiritual community that doesn't include people who are just like me. I want to be in communion with people older and younger, with those of differing backgrounds and diverse interpretations of the holy. I want to worship next to them and hear their voices blend with mine as we sing and pray. I want to be reminded when we gather that I'm not the only one walking this path of the spirit, what my Lakota friends call the Red Road.

During those months I also discovered that I wanted to remain a deacon. I missed preaching, the playing with metaphors for the holy and the captive audience to hear my ruminations. I missed standing in the middle of the congregation to read the Gospel, reciting those ancient stories of loss and redemption and miracles.

In the end, the most powerful lure that brought me back into the Christian fold was receiving communion. At the Church of God's Odds and Ends, they add an element I'd never experienced before: as people approach the altar, they dip their fingers into the water of the baptismal font and then make the sign of the cross on the forehead of the person behind them. This simple ritual is repeated over and over again. It soon became my favorite part of the service, watching as a five-year-old reaches up to make the sign of the cross on the forehead of a grown man, who turns around to make it on the lined forehead of a woman in her 80s, one after another, so that all the odds and ends of the congregation get woven into a whole.

Each week after I'd done this ritual, I approached the altar. As a small piece of bread was given to me, the priest smiled, looked into my eyes with great kindness, and said, "Lori, this is the body of Christ, the bread of heaven."

The body of Christ, the bread of heaven. I was beginning to sense the tide of faith returning.

∾

After a half-year on sabbatical, I officially resigned from All Saints and became a deacon once again, this time at the Church of God's Odds and Ends. My first Sunday back at the altar came just before Christmas. I'd chosen the Sunday at random, because the other deacon was singing in the choir that day and our son Carl was home for the holiday and it just felt like it was time. I put on the robe I hadn't worn for months, and at the beginning of the service walked up to the altar beside the priest, as I'd done hundreds of times at All Saints.

All morning I'd been distracted by being back in the diaconal saddle again, trying to remember details like how to set the altar for communion and when to start the Prayers of the People. At one point early in the service, I realized I needed to glance over the Gospel reading, just in case it had any words I might stumble over. When I saw the passage, I smiled.

Carl Jung said the divine speaks to us in synchronicities, the seemingly random but interconnected occurrences that give a glimpse of the underlying order of the universe. The coincidence that morning was that the Gospel reading happened to be my favorite passage in the entire Bible: the Magnificat, the glorious hymn that Mary sings at the very beginning of the Christmas story.

How appropriate, I thought. I'm going to love reading those words.

A few minutes later, I was standing in the middle of the congregation, an acolyte holding the Gospel book open for me, its pages turned to the right passage. I began reading with a clear and confident voice:

And Mary said,
"My soul magnifies the Lord,
   and my spirit rejoices in God my Savior,
for he has looked with favor on the lowliness of his servant.

Then I stopped, because suddenly I was overwhelmed by emotion. I knew that if I read any further, I'd cry. The silence grew, and as the seconds passed it felt like time and space were expanding, enfolding all of us in something that I can only describe as holiness. I could feel people's eyes on me, and I sensed the love that radiated from their faces, the *agape* that doesn't mean you have to know someone well, just that you're willing to walk with them on the Red Road.

I was a little embarrassed, frankly, because the silence was stretching on for a long time. But mainly I was so thankful to be there, right where I was supposed to be.

And then Mary, who always comes through just when you need her, continued with the rest of her song. It was my voice, wavering and cracking, but she was there, speaking the words through me:

   Surely, from now on all generations will call me blessed;
for the Mighty One has done great things for me,
   and holy is his name.
His mercy is for those who fear him
   from generation to generation.
He has shown strength with his arm;
   he has scattered the proud in the thoughts of their hearts.

He has brought down the powerful from their thrones,
*   and lifted up the lowly;*
He has filled the hungry with good things,
*   and sent the rich away empty.*
He has helped his servant Israel,
*   in remembrance of his mercy,*
according to the promise he made to our ancestors,
*   to Abraham and to his descendants forever."*

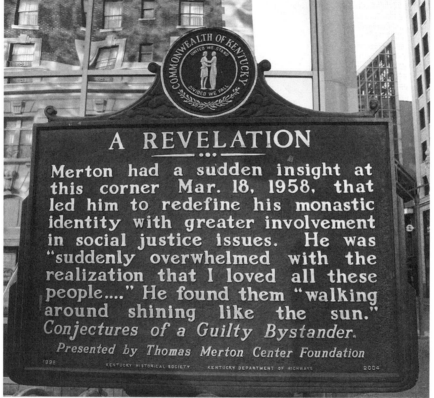

A REVELATION

Merton had a sudden insight at this corner Mar. 18, 1958, that led him to redefine his monastic identity with greater involvement in social justice issues. He was "suddenly overwhelmed with the realization that I loved all these people...." He found them "walking around shining like the sun." *Conjectures of a Guilty Bystander.*

Presented by Thomas Merton Center Foundation

KENTUCKY HISTORICAL SOCIETY   KENTUCKY DEPARTMENT OF HIGHWAYS   2004

Thomas Merton historical marker in Louisville, Kentucky

EPILOGUE

VISIONS

On March 18, 1958, Thomas Merton was in Louisville, Kentucky, running errands for his monastery. In the middle of that ordinary day he had a mystical vision, which he would later describe in *Conjectures of a Guilty Bystander*:

> In Louisville, at the corner of Fourth and Walnut, in the center of the shopping district, I was suddenly overwhelmed with the realization that I loved all those people, that they were mine and I theirs, that we could not be alien to one another even though we were total strangers. It was like waking from a dream of separateness, of spurious self-isolation in a special world, the world of renunciation and supposed holiness. The whole illusion of a separate holy existence is a dream. . . . There is no way of telling people that they are all walking around shining like the sun. . . . I suddenly saw the secret beauty of their hearts, the depths of their hearts where neither sin nor desire nor self-knowledge can reach, the core of their reality, the person that each one is in God's eyes. If only they could all see themselves as they really are. If only we could see each other that way all the time.

On the corner of Fourth and Walnut Streets today is a bronze plaque describing Merton's experience—as far as I know, the only historical marker commemorating a mystical vision in the United States.

That vision changed Merton's life. Up until that point he'd seen himself as separate from the world, someone removed from the rest of humanity by his status as a monk. But after his experience in downtown Louisville, he realized he was connected to everyone else and that God doesn't make favorites of those who've taken religious vows. From this epiphany came his re-engagement with the world, his writings about social justice, and his reaching beyond the monastery walls to connect with seekers of many kinds.

When I stood on that street corner and read the plaque, it brought to mind an experience of my own, a pilgrimage more important than any other I've described in this book.

It took place shortly after my return to Christianity. With the zeal of a new convert, I'd scheduled a silent retreat at a center run by a religious community in the rural Midwest. I'm not going to tell where it is, because I don't recommend anyone go there. The place had forlorn, rundown buildings and a staff who appeared to have done very little of their spiritual homework.

I came to this place with my friend Cindy, but we'd agreed to remain apart the entire three days, each in our own private hermitage in the woods. I hadn't brought any reading material along other than a Bible and a prayer book, thinking that I'd be spending all my time in contemplation.

This lasted about an hour. Then I grew increasingly frustrated, and after 24 hours, I was nearly out of my mind with boredom.

It helped when I discovered that if I walked very slowly, a stroll around the property could take nearly an hour. The highlight of each day was picking up my meals, which were left in a box at a central location. I brought them back to my cabin, where I tried to stretch out the chewing as long as possible.

If I'd been on my own I'd certainly have left, but I was stuck because of being there with Cindy. I imagined her sitting in her cabin across the road, absorbed in prayer and meditation, glancing up occasionally to marvel at the sunlight streaming through the window. Envy did not improve my mood.

My third night there, I went to sleep early and was awakened around 4:00 a.m. by rustling and banging outside my front door. I'd left a can of soda pop outside to get cool, and it sounded like some woodland creature was investigating it (the next morning I deduced it was a raccoon from the footprints it left in the mud—apparently no bears were in the area to do the job of waking me up). Once I was awake, I couldn't get back to sleep.

I lay in bed, staring at the ceiling and counting the hours until I'd be able to leave.

I'd pretty much exhausted every other subject to think about, so I started reviewing my entire life. I recalled my childhood, my student years, my time as a young wife and mother. I wondered if my perpetual spiritual quest was nothing more than wishful thinking or narcissism. I thought of the times when my path could have gone in a variety of directions, when I'd made a choice that sent me down a fork in the road, which in turn branched out to another. Perhaps those were the points where my life had intersected with the divine.

And then, something shifted. For the briefest of moments, I saw something that I'm going to do my best to explain, though once again I have the problem of trying to write about something that can't be put into words.

What I saw was this: all of the people who love me have the face of God. Each day of my life I'd seen God's face, but I'd been totally oblivious to it.

This may sound sweet and sentimental, but instead the sight was so overwhelming that I felt like I'd been hit in the chest by a hard blow. I sat up in bed, gasping for air, my heart pounding.

I remained there for perhaps an hour, watching as the dawn slowly filled the sky outside my window, the adrenalin gradually dissipating as I went over and over again in my mind what I'd experienced.

The poet William Blake has a line that I think helps explain what I saw, and what Thomas Merton witnessed on the street corner in Louisville, and what countless other mystics and pilgrims in many traditions have experienced through the centuries. "We are put on earth . . . that we may learn to bear the beams of love," Blake said. I think what he meant is that the power of divine love is so strong and so brilliant that as humans we cannot fully comprehend it and must be shielded from its full force.

On my wanderings around the world, I've searched for this radiance, never again experiencing it with such force, but nevertheless seeing hints of it in many places. Luther, Thoreau, Bernadette, Merton, Hildegard, and Columba have helped guide me on my way. I've sensed this light on Helgafell in Iceland, in the House of the Virgin Mary in Ephesus, on a hillside in Galilee, and in a Buddhist temple in Indiana. I felt its presence on the side of a mountain at Machu Picchu and on Bear Butte. It shone from Rich's face as he died and on Owen's as he came back to life.

It's the divine light breaking through, and it blazes so brightly we can only bear it in small glimpses.

✎

Finally released from the prison of my hermitage, I joined up with Cindy later that morning. I knew she was trained as a spiritual director, and I was eager to hear her opinion of what I'd experienced. I poured out my story to her over coffee at McDonald's, the prosaic setting contrasting with the tale I was telling her. Already the memory of the luminescence that had nearly blinded me was fading, but at the same time I didn't know how I could have imagined it.

At the end I asked, "Did I actually see what I thought I did?"

"You won't know for a long time," she said. "You'll know it was real if it changes your life."

From the perspective of years, I can say this: my life was changed. And I think what I experienced was real.

ACKNOWLEDGMENTS

This book is the fruit of the warm welcome I received in holy sites around the world and the loving fellowship of the faith communities described within these pages. I'm grateful to all of the people who've been companions on my spiritual journeys.

Jacquelyn Phillips, the Jackie of this book, inspired and influenced me in countless ways. Her legacy continues in the work of many healers, including Lisa Bormann, beloved by both Jackie and me.

I'm grateful to have had Rich Oberfoell, a man of rare courage and joie de vivre, as one of my dearest friends. And I'm thankful to Rich's family for allowing me to tell part of the story of his remarkable life in this book. Sun Hee, Carol, and Xavier continue to inspire me with their strength and love.

My friends in the Midwest Travel Journalists Association and the Society of American Travel Writers have been wonderful traveling companions on adventures around the world—especially Sue Pollack, Rich Warren, Mary Bergin, and Susan Dallas. Thanks also to my photographer friends whose images grace this book: Eric Lindberg, Ellen Clark, and David Noyes (as well as Bob Sessions, my extraordinary photographer-philosopher-handyman husband).

I give a deep bow of gratitude to the Venerable Arjia Rinpoche for his welcome and wisdom, and to Lisa Morrison, who introduced me to the Bloomington Tibetan Buddhist community.

Jim Stands and Sylvan White Hat taught me about Lakota ways in the best way possible: through hospitality and stories. *Mitakuye oyasin.*

My blog, Holy Rover, provided the spark that became this book. Darcy Lipsius and Marian Wingo kept me writing when hardly anyone else was reading my work. I'm especially grateful to Marian for inviting me to Turkey and for support in matters large and small, and to Darcy for teaching me about Mary, among many other important things.

Barb Lewis, Friend Extraordinaire, served as midwife for this manuscript, editing multiple drafts, prodding me to improve it, and making me laugh with her irreverent marginal comments. And Rebecca Christian Patience has provided me with a model for living, as well as writing, for nearly four decades.

I'm grateful to Jan Locher for asking the question that launched this book, to Susan Lutgendorf for the many walks during which we discussed the events and ideas within it, to Connie Mutel for the use of her beautiful house and woods as a writing retreat, and to Jennifer Masada and Julia Easley for tending my soul. Catherine Quehl-Engel has been my valued partner-in-pilgrimage, and Chris Vinsonhaler has challenged me to think more deeply about nearly everything, including the Iowa State Fair.

Thanks also to these companions on the Spiritual Highway: Sarah McGrew, Lindy Weilgart, Ellyn Waterbury, Mel and Barbara Schlachter, Marc Haack, Chris Kellerman, Steve Locher, Dick and Debra Dorzweiler, Wendelin Guentner, Brian Witzke, Bill Blair, Julia Mears, Andrea Billhardt, Janet Freeman, Annechien Dik, Michael Baxter, Intesar Duncan, and Cindy Schmidt. And to the irrepressible Wild Women of the Wilderness (who include Ilona Lichty, Susan White, and Brenda Nations, as well as several WWWs mentioned above): thanks for always being in my corner.

I think all faith communities should have a ministry in Healing Touch. For information on how to make that happen, see Healing Beyond Borders (www.healingbeyondborders.org).

I'm grateful to my editor, Tony Jones, the staff of Fortress Press, and my agent, Greg Daniel. They helped make this a better book, though all errors and heresies contained within it are entirely my own responsibility.

Finally, I owe a large debt of gratitude to my family for their love and support. My parents, Myron and Grace Erickson, gave me deep roots in Iowa soil, and my sister, Julie Fahlin, helped me remember what I'd forgotten. And I honor with love the memory of my brother, Alan.

Most of all, I'm grateful to the three men who are my most treasured companions on my journey through life: Owen, Carl, and Bob Sessions. Wherever I roam, their love sustains me.

ENDNOTES

Opening poem credit: William Stafford, "The Way It Is" from *Ask Me: 100 Essential Poems*. Copyright © 1998, 2014 by William Stafford and the Estate of William Stafford. Reprinted with the permission of The Permissions Company, Inc. on behalf of Graywolf Press, Minneapolis, Minnesota, www.graywolfpress.org.

page xv, "Today, perhaps, the mournful . . ." Stoddard, *John L. Stoddard's Lectures*, Vol. VI, 178

page 5, "I believe in the Holy Spirit . . ." Apostle's Creed, *Praying Together: English Language Liturgical Consultation*, 22

page 19, "Any act based on . . ." Starhawk, *The Spiral Dance: A Rebirth of the Ancient Religion of the Great Goddess*, 84

page 24, "What have you deserved . . ." Luther, *Small Catechism*

page 25, "The Goddess is not separate . . ." Starhawk, *The Spiral Dance: A Rebirth of the Ancient Religion of the Great Goddess*, 8

page 84, Parable of the Lost Son, Luke: 15:11–32

page 87, "From the moment I first saw the poster . . ." Nouwen, *The Return of the Prodigal Son: A Story of Homecoming*, 96

page 101, "All at once, without warning . . ." James, *The Varieties of Religious Experience,* 390

page 113, "In one sense we are . . ." Thomas P. McDonnell, editor, *A Thomas Merton Reader*, 513

Page 114, "I began to haunt . . ." Merton, *The Seven Storey Mountain*, 120

page 116–17, "Contemplation is the highest . . ." Merton, *New Seeds of Con templation*, 1

page 119, "Even when I cannot think . . ." Merton, *The Sign of Jonas*, 75

page 139, "I am merely a . . ." Carmen Acevedo Butcher, *St. Hildegard of Bingen: Doctor of the Church*, 61–62

page 143, "This is the perception of God's . . ." Hildegard of Bingen, *Scivias*, 161

page 156, "As you are outwardly anointed . . ." *Book of Common Prayer*, 456

page 163, "Hardly had we left . . ." Bingham, *Lost City of the Incas*, 151

page 198, "Chaos should be regarded . . ." Chödrön, *When Things Fall Apart: Heart Advice for Difficult Times,* xiv; "When everything falls apart . . ." Chödrön, 86

Page 199, "Everything that ends . . ." Chödrön, 79

page 217, "We stole away because . . ." Bradley, *The Celtic Way*, 80

page 223–24, "And Mary said, My soul . . ." Luke 1:46–55, Credit: New Revised Standard Version Bible, copyright © 1989 National Council of the Churches of Christ in the United States of America. Used by permission. All rights reserved.

page 227, "In Louisville, at the corner of . . ." Merton, *Conjectures of a Guilty Bystander*, 153–54